Library Of Small Happiness

Also By Leslie Ullman

Natural Histories
Dreams By No One's Daughter
Slow Work Through Sand
Progress On The Subject Of Immensity

Library Of Small Happiness

Essays, Poems, And Exercises On The Craft Of Poetry

LESLIE ULLMAN

ʒ

Three: A Taos Press

Book Design & Typesetting: Lesley Cox, FEEL Design Associates, Taos, NM

Press Logo Design: William Watson, Castro Watson, New York, NY

Front Cover Artwork: Jean Siméon Chardin, *Soap Bubbles*, oil on canvas, 1733/1734, National Gallery of Art, Washington, D.C., Gift of Mrs. John W. Simpson

Author Photograph: Jim O'Donnell, Taos, NM

Text Typeset in Stempel Schneidler

Printed in the United States of America by Cottrell Printing Company

ISBN: 978-0-9972011-2-3

3: A Taos Press
P.O. Box 370627
Denver, CO 80237
www.3taospress.com

10 9 8 7 6 5 4 3 2 1

In gratitude to my students and colleagues at University of Texas-El Paso, whose openness encouraged me for many years to open in return. And to my students and colleagues at Vermont College of the Fine Arts, whose friendship and accomplishment continue to nudge and nourish me—I can't imagine what my writing-and-thinking life would have been without you.

CONTENTS

Preface

I. ESSAYS

17   A "Dark Star" Passes Through It

35   Towards A Poetics Of Pull-And-Release: Some Thoughts
     On Silence In Poems

55   A Meditation On Place, Real And Imagined

63   The "Personal" Poem As Sacred Space

89   A Spiral Walk Through The Golden Mean

105 "All The Softness Truth Requires:" Speculation
     As Invitation And Persuasion

121 Press Send: Risk, Intuition, And The Transparent Poem

II. EXERCISES

147 The Poetic Inversion

155 From Nymph To Elder: Beyond The Viability Of Seduction

165 First Lines By Others: A Leap Into Fruitful Spaces

171 Juxtaposition And The Gifts of Brilliant Surprise: The Braided Poem

177 Estrangement And Reconciliation: The Self Has It Out
     With The Self

183 Notes On Revision

189 References

195 Bibliography

199 Acknowledgments

201 Permissions

205 About The Author

207 Also By 3: A Taos Press

PREFACE:

THE ESSAY THAT FAILED

*M*y apprenticeship as a thinker, reader, and essayist began long ago, before I went to graduate school in order to determine whether or not I was a poet. Even in high school, I performed best when given the occasional open-ended essay assignment that allowed me to invent my own wheel, using the materials at hand, rather than demonstrate knowledge picked up from lectures and textbooks. In college, I felt more at home in my two creative writing classes—poetry and writing for magazines—than I did in any class where I had to take tests. After college, for a while, I embarked on a career as a magazine editor and tried to keep writing poetry between the seams of a nine-to-five schedule.

In the early 1970's, I entered the Iowa Writers Workshop where, luckily, I was left alone—to write poems, to write "personal intellectual" responses to the literature I read, and to engage in dialogues with my frighteningly accomplished classmates. In dialogue with my own journal one day, I surprised myself by writing this:

Unlike so many others here, I seem to absorb the energy and general shape of a piece of thinking/writing at a level that is undetectable at first. I come away with bold outlines, an unarticulated grasp of impulses and implications, which settle in some subterranean place until a discussion or other point of focus draws them out again. Then, they appear in terms and contexts quite different from the ones I found them in. My aptitude seems to lie in the translation of ideas. The ability to make leaps outward from a source. Increasingly, I'm aware that I carry with me an approach rather than a background of knowledge, so that anything I say in a given situation is called forth as a response to something else. The existence of my ideas depends on the existence of that *something*. If I never found myself in dialogues with others, I would not know I had ideas at all.

Dialogue proved crucial in more expansive ways when I began teaching workshops and literature classes several years later—dialogue with original texts, with published texts, and especially with students. I was rarely inclined to lecture, and when I did so, the impulse rose in response to a question or craft issue that recently had come up in class. Far more fruitful for me were questions. If I could get students talking, I knew I would be able to reach into myself and teach well; thus did I feel my way into the Socratic Method. And this resulted in discoveries that led me to teach literature differently from the ways I had been taught—discoveries that prompted me to write, two years into my tenure-track position, what I have come to call *The Essay That Failed*. It was a sprawling thing, repetitive and at times preachy, a wheel that invented itself multiple times to the point of dissolution—a dialogue that never quite determined just who was on the other side. Looking back, I think I may have been arguing with my own background. But more important, I began to articulate ideas about teaching literature, especially poems, in response to the friendly skepticism of two of my colleagues, one a Medievalist and one a Milton scholar, who were suspicious of creative writing as a viable field but who loved dialogue more than they loved being right.

Essentially, the essay served as rite of passage, allowing me to define what kind of thinker and teacher I was coming to be, and how I was getting there. I have salvaged the following passage to show my point of departure:

> Most of us who are avid readers probably acquire that avidity early in our literate lives, before we have had much intellectual experience or any intellectual discipline. At that stage, to sit down and read means simply to be transported by that work beyond ourselves. Later, when works of literature become objects of study, we are encouraged to learn another kind of readerly experience, that of stepping somewhat outside the work in order to determine the writer's intentions. The thinking *inside* the work, then, becomes a less self-contained, less resonant phenomenon, and consequently the reader herself becomes less self-contained, more a representative of the "world" to which the writer supposedly intends to speak. In this transaction, the intensity of the reading experience is channeled, at least in part, from its pure experiential form into the realm of idea, of detachable and shareable truths.

This distinction, which I made in 1981, looks dated to me now. But along with a few other aspects of *The Essay That Failed,* it continued to resonate for me and informed my approach to every class and workshop I taught, and my approach to language in every review and essay I wrote about poetry, in the years that followed. This is the crux:

I have learned to guide students into the tasks of analysis and writing by treating poems as experiences to which the student first brings, then deepens, her own experiences as a thinking being. "Craft," "form," "logic," and "specificity" remain important terms in our discussions, but mainly as they serve to clarify the thought process of the reader herself as she confronts the thought process in another's work. To treat a poem as an occasion for experience complete in itself requires from the reader a personal inquiry into the nature of that experience; it is to ask, "What is happening to me through it?" before asking, "What is this about?"

This approach, as it invites significant participation on the part of the reader, has helped me to move as an essayist beyond a purely subjective response into a critically astute one when analysis has been the task of an essay or review. In other pieces, especially the six longer essays that make up the backbone of this book, the experiential approach itself often has been or has heavily informed the subject at hand. The arena in which the reader not only participates, but determines *how* she will participate, is what I have come to call "the sacred space" that poems offer us, a silence that resonates with the presence of two voices, only one of which is the writer's.

While the essays in this collection address a variety of poetry-related subjects that include craft issues, critical analysis, personal accompaniments to published poems, and writing exercises, I see in retrospect that dialogue in some form underlies every single one of them: with others' poems, with my students' concerns, with the mysterious workings of process, and with language itself once a writing prompt results in a few tentative phrases and speculations committed to a page. I have included a sprinkling of my own poems as well, and these are meant as invitations rather than performances—templates or catalysts for writers to use in service to their own inventions.

My early recognition that I could discover my own ideas when prompted by others' ideas has borne fine fruit in the sense that, early on, I was liberated from the need to do it all myself. And from the need to sound academic, to satisfy an editor by second-guessing what he or she might want, or by looking over my shoulder to see how others had done a similar task. Re-inventing the wheel can be a recipe for falling on one's face, as I have learned more than once. But it can also keep alive the excitement of beginning an essay as though beginning a journey and feeling something more than just one's intellect reaching towards others. As I have reviewed and arranged these pieces written during years of dialogues with poems, students, and peers, I have come to recognize that this book, which is about poetry, is even more about collaboration between imagination and the written word.

I.
Essays

A "DARK STAR" PASSES THROUGH IT

*A*n inspired, well-made poem is all muscle, all linked movement and harmonious gestures, efficient and lovely as a snake moving across rocks or blacktop or water before it disappears into tall grass. Break this good poem down, and one can see it as a construct of images, phrases, observations, maybe even statements—gestures which have practical uses and varying levels of energy when taken one at a time. Often these gestures are indeed taken one at a time, in workshops or in classrooms at any level, where "understanding" the poem is a more graspable and thus a more settled-for goal than *feeling* the poem. Start discussing feeling, and one is in that no-man's land where the boundaries between one's private experience of the poem and the intentions of the poem can blur. Language becomes untrustworthy. Perception becomes suspect. It is one thing to watch a snake move and imagine its slipperiness; it is quite another to pick it up with an ungloved hand and then sustain and communicate to someone else the sensations of smooth muscle against the palm—at least in the arena of a workshop or literature class, where the task is to find usable terms and defend a point of view in the midst of peers and teachers. But in private, one might well pick up the snake, find one's hand and arm moving in a dance with its body, and feel the marvelous interlocking of its sinews and scales, the dry smoothness of it, not a slipperiness at all.

My first experience of the quietly electrifying impact a poem can have occurred when I was sitting alone on a dock one summer before my junior year in college. Since then, I have sought ways to honor what can scarcely be described about a well-made and deeply inspired poem—the vatic sureness, the textured play of utterance and silence, the sense of inevitability or urgency from which a poem seems to arise, the resonance some images have, the way the last line reverberates in the reader's mind and sends her back into the poem again and again only to find each reading richer than the last. In graduate school, I was introduced to the work of Gaston Bachelard, the French phenomenologist and philosopher of science who understood *reverberation* as the operative word for describing the dynamics of literary expression, emphasizing the wealth of association and memory touched off in the reader, often a recognition of something deeply buried within herself, as part of a literary work's own properties and realm of intentions. Bachelard helped me take seriously the *sensations* that arise from inspired reading, the literal twinges in the gut that tell me when I have encountered a particularly important image or passage even before my head tells me why it's important. A few years later, a conversation with my then-colleague James Ragan helped me begin to find a vocabulary for including and then using sensation as a starting point for grasping the whole of a poem, its deft and muscular movement, in a way that might appeal to readers at any level of experience.

Over the years, I have played with the notion of a poem's "center" in so many contexts as a teacher, and thus have made it so deeply my own, that I can no longer determine how much of what I have to say on this matter originates with me or with Jim. But I can say that the basic idea came from him, and that when he introduced it to me, a light went on in my head and has stayed on ever since. Jim said, if I remember correctly, that every poem has a "center," a line or group of lines, which reveal the heart of the poem but should not be confused with theme or content. Rather, they are lines with a particular sort of energy, almost always a heightened energy. And that one way to identify them is to imagine the writer feeling, once she drafted these particular lines, the force and trajectory of the finished poem even if many details still needed to be worked out—that the poem from that time forward held mystery and potential completeness for the writer and would indeed be worth finishing. I loved this. To enter a poem in the skin of the writer, to feel the itch of important lines without quite yet knowing what they mean—this seemed an engaging and intuitively accurate way to be a reader.

I soon discovered that one cannot identify a poem's center without dwelling within each of a poem's gestures—each image, each transition, each close-up or wide-angle view—without, in other words, feeling the weave of the entire texture, its larger and smaller variations. This is not the work of intellect or analysis. Imagine being blindfolded, learning the layout of a room by groping your way along its walls and furnishings, letting your sense of touch replace your eyes and yield the landscape of the room in a visceral, intimate way. This is what happens when one reads a poem with the intent of identifying its center. The center derives its energy from how it works in its relation to other moments in the poem. To feel the center of a poem, one has to have felt the significance of *all* of the poem's moments, moments of lesser as well as greater intensity that nevertheless are crucial to the poem's structure and cumulative power. This is what picking up the snake—not the devious Edenic archetype, but the lovely work of nature—is all about.

The center can occur anywhere in the poem. It can be a phrase or a stanza, or it may reveal its energy in the gap between stanzas. It can be a moment where the poem's tension is most palpably enacted, where the poem's time frames or layers interact simultaneously, where the texture of the poem undergoes significant variation, where the poem contradicts itself, or where the poem seems to quicken and gather itself into a passage

A "Dark Star"
Passes Through It

19

that acts as a kind of net. The center is where the reader feels most powerfully the *sensations* of the poem's theme. And nearly always, the center contains a pivot or surprise that gives the whole poem simultaneous light and darkness, hence considerable range.

I call these moments "dark star" moments, after an image in a beautifully crafted poem by James Tate titled *Consumed*. This poem manages, through apparently conventional rhetorical gestures of question and answer, elaboration on that answer and then conclusion, to catapult the reader into a state of uncertainty that is bracing, absolute, and utterly resistant to paraphrase:

Consumed

Why should you believe in magic,
pretend an interest in astrology
or the tarot? Truth is, you are

free, and what might happen to you
today, nobody knows. And your
personality may undergo a radical

transformation in the next half
hour. So it goes. You are consumed
by your faith in justice, your

hope for a better day, the rightness
of fate, the dreams, the lies,
the taunts. —Nobody gets what he

wants. A dark star passes through
you on your way home from
the grocery: never again are you

the same—an experience which is
impossible to forget, impossible
to share. The longing to be pure

is over. You are the stranger
who gets stranger by the hour.[1]

The poem begins reasonably enough, with a progression of statements which set up an argument against the possibility of solace, of safe
illusions. Then it heats up in the third and fourth stanzas as it launches
into a list that starts with "faith in justice" and ends bluntly with "taunts."
The list gathers speed as it progresses and ultimately achieves, through its
movement towards self-cancellation, a sensation of downward spiraling
that slides into the abrupt, oddly punctuated statement, "—Nobody gets
what he wants," which at this point feels both jolting and inevitable. Then
comes the poem's single image, resonant with conflicting energies: "A dark
star passes through/you on your way home from/the grocery." The mysterious arrival of the "dark star" occurs at the end of a mundane trip to the
grocery, enacting what the poem has been saying about one's absolute vulnerability to the unexpected. But also, at a more visceral level, the words
"dark" and "star" work against each other to create immediate friction in
their simultaneous assertions of darkness and light. Following that passage,
then, the poem becomes more outrageous, more unrelenting in its depic-
tions of human vulnerability, returning to its former strategy of making
statements, but making them work as a quick succession of hammer blows
to set up a no-win situation. The arrival of the "dark star" is "impossible to
forget, impossible/to share," and once the hapless "you" in the poem has
been jolted from complacency, there is no turning back or even slowing
down in this free-fall towards uncertainty: "You are the stranger/who gets
stranger by the hour."

Because of the provocative leaps between its statements, and because it layers paradox upon paradox, *Consumed* evokes the sensation of being swept into a vortex. For me, it creates, with economy and brilliance, a black hole. I can scarcely contemplate a black hole as a palpable phenomenon even though I can feel myself heading into one in this poem, and the image of the "dark star"—also a scarcely graspable physical reality—seems a perfect emblem for such an experience. At many levels then, "A dark star passes through/you on your way home from/the grocery" is a viable center to this poem: it marks a turning point, it offers a significant variation in the poem's texture as the sole image among rhetorical gestures, and it captures the poem's self-contradictory energy in an instant, forcing us to experience a deeply interior moment through an image from the most extreme imaginable version of the outer world, the cosmos and its mysterious alchemies. The "dark star," after all, arises from the universe within, without warning or cause. How bracing. How perverse. The explosive domain of the Existentialists is crystallized in this tiny jewel of a poem.

Such play of simultaneous light and darkness is a condensed form of the tension that gives form and urgency to any literary work. In fiction and drama, we look for the tension/resolution dynamic between the protagonist and whatever forces work against her; how that tension is established and then resolved becomes more or less the basis of plot structure. Poems, especially lyric poems, usually work around a brief period of time, sometimes only a moment, to illuminate a certain complexity therein, relying not on a sequence of events or elements, but rather suspending them in a matrix of memory, present event, and reflection in such a way as to reveal new relationships between them. At the end of a work of fiction and drama, we usually experience a sense of *resolution*, but lyric poems leave us with a more open-ended sense of *revelation*. The poem's center provides the key to the tension that leads to revelation, indicating the area where the surface is ruffled and the underlying shadows have more noticeable play. The search for a center is especially useful in nudging the reader into the trickier depths of poems that at first appear, unlike Tate's intentionally disturbing poem, to be neutral or even celebratory.

Here, for example, is a poem by Mary Oliver, whose nature poems risk a lack of tension as they arise from a sensibility that is not ironic, not critical, not humorous, not agendized in any way but is simply, "devotional," as she elsewhere has described it:

Beside the Waterfall

At dawn
           the big dog—
           Winston by name—
     reached down

into the leaves—tulips and willows mostly—
           beside the white
           waterfall,
               and dragged out,

into plain sight,
           a fawn;
               it was scarcely larger
                   than a rabbit

and, thankfully,
           it was dead.
            Winston
               looked over the

delicate, spotted body and then
           deftly
              tackled
                  the beautiful flower-like head,

breaking it and

breaking it off and

swallowing it.

All the while this was happening

it was growing lighter.

When I called to him

Winston merely looked up.

Grizzled around the chin

and with kind eyes,

he, too, if you're willing,

had a face

like a flower; and then the red sun,

which had been rising all the while anyway,

broke

clear of the trees and dropped its wild, clawed light

over everything.[2]

The elegance and restraint with which Oliver describes this brutal scene does much to supply the poem's tension. Only at the end does she allow her voice to reveal something of a reaction when she mentions the sun's "wild, clawed light," as though her faithful rendition of details up to this point finally has forced her into an image that conveys the thrust and music of raw feeling. But on the way, there are two areas where the poem quietly heats up, and these qualify as possible "centers." The first is the fifth stanza, where the language Oliver uses to describe the dog's act evokes a sense of daintiness and even loveliness: "delicate, spotted body," "deftly," and "beautiful flower-like head." The word "tackled" works in counterpoint to remind us this is real violence, the dark side of nature brought to light and then rendered beautiful through Oliver's diction and detail. This is the stuff of centers.

But I believe the real center occurs in the poem's second-to-last stanza, where the dog looks up from his meal "with kind eyes" and the poet sees that "he, too, if you're willing,/had a face/like a flower... ." At that point, the poem gathers all its elements into one intensely visual instant: the flower-faces of both predator and prey, the sun's red light (of course there's blood, but it never needs to be mentioned), and the deft reminder that there is nothing evil—nothing, after all, that is not "kind," even though suggestive of seemingly dark acts—in this scene. While the first section I mentioned begins to gather them, here is where all the elements of the poem rush together as though through a funnel to become energetically fused, and full of dark light. This moment underscores another dynamic that contributes to the poem's overall tension, the consummation of this "dark" moment just as the sun crests the horizon at dawn.

James Wright's well-known poem, *Lying in a Hammock at William Duffy's Farm in Pine Island, Minnesota*, a poem which also seems to celebrate nature, offers an example of yet another way in which a center can be identified as the point of tension:

Lying in a Hammock at William Duffy's Farm
in Pine Island, Minnesota

Over my head, I see the bronze butterfly,
Asleep on the black trunk,
Blowing like a leaf in green shadow.
Down the ravine behind the empty house,
The cowbells follow one another
Into the distances of the afternoon.
To my right,
In a field of sunlight between two pines,
The droppings of last year's horses
Blaze up into golden stones.
I lean back, as the evening darkens and comes on.
A chicken hawk floats over, looking for home.
I have wasted my life.[3]

This enigmatic yet graspable final line has caused Wright's poem to be the subject of much debate in classrooms. Has the speaker wasted his life by not spending more time lying in a hammock and observing the natural world so closely? Or have his observations led him into a confrontation of a certain aimlessness to his life, a tendency to remain in a hammock instead of doing other things? There are clues throughout the poem to support both of these interpretations. Someone who sees old droppings as "golden stones" could be speaking from a pleasurably heightened sensitivity to his surroundings and perhaps celebrating a moment of freedom from the noise of the world. But the chicken hawk "looking for home" suggests the possibility that the speaker is himself feeling ungrounded, absent from some sense of home in himself, as he projects this interesting interpretation on a bird in flight. If that image had occurred earlier in the poem, it might have been absorbed and rendered neutral, but here it takes on a higher charge as it provides the closest thing we have to a springboard for the final, startling line. This is a classic example of how epiphany works in a poem, arriving as an outgrowth or a summary of what has come before, but doing so through an associative leap that leaves gaps for the reader to fill in. Upon subsequent readings, she can begin to feel the links of feeling within the poem, the particular resonance of each image or moment as it might relate to that final utterance. This is participatory reading at its best. The poem turns on itself, and the reader is catapulted back to the beginning. A surprising, well-contexted epiphany is almost always the center of any poem that contains one.

The center of a poem may be identified differently by different readers. When I ask students to look for a center, I am really asking them to roll up their sleeves and plunge their hands in up to the elbows, feel the interaction between the poem's elements, and then defend their choices articulately. If they argue with one another, if they disagree with my own choice, it's all to the good as long as the exercise has encouraged them to read the poem energetically and with a reasonable degree of accuracy.

It is often tempting, for example, to identify a favorite image or stanza as the center, so here I reiterate that the center is defined by its relationship to all the other moments in the poem, whereas an especially resonant image derives its energy partly from the friction or connection between elements within it, but partly also from the associations it touches off in the reader's mind. To a certain degree, we all bring our own daydreaming selves into another's poem, and this is a fruitful and legitimate way to live with poems. Bachelard maintains that poems arise from *reverie*, a state of mind that is at once alert and "in repose," subconscious but not in the repressive Freudian sense, rich with memory and association, and that the poet's reverie touches off a similar state of mind in the reader. This, I think, is sacred space, a personal dialogue between reader and poem, and it should not be violated by the injunction to explain or interpret a poem to someone else's satisfaction. Still, anyone who teaches poetry to inexperienced readers knows that the poem's own space can be violated by too subjective a reading, and that a well-made poem gives all the necessary clues to someone who knows how to look for them. To seek the center is to learn to recognize those clues with greater ease. To acknowledge the other hot spots, the other points for pause and reflection, is to honor the more personal dialectic between poem and reader. If the search for a poem's center involves a discussion of both kinds of response, so much the better.

While most centers can be characterized at least in part by their heightened energy, as they have in the three poems discussed (i.e., a highly charged image, a forceful gathering of a poem's elements, and provocative juxtaposition), occasionally a center manifests itself more gently, without visible exertion of energy. In the center of the following poem by William Stafford, the language becomes a little more discursive, a shade less concrete, than it is elsewhere in the poem:

A "Dark Star"
Passes Through It

27

Traveling Through the Dark

Traveling through the dark I found a deer
dead on the edge of the Wilson River road.
It is usually best to roll them into the canyon:
that road is narrow; to swerve might make more dead.

By the glow of the tail-light I stumbled back of the car
and stood by the heap, a doe, a recent killing;
she had stiffened already, almost cold.
I dragged her off; she was large in the belly.

My fingers touching her side brought me the reason—
her side was warm; her fawn lay there waiting,
alive, still, never to be born.
Beside that mountain road I hesitated.

The car aimed ahead its lowered parking lights;
under the hood purred the steady engine.
I stood in the glare of the warm exhaust turning red;
around our group I could hear the wilderness listen.

I thought hard for us all—my only swerving—
then pushed her over the edge into the river.[4]

It is tempting to zero in on that fawn "waiting,/alive, still, never to be born," an image that throbs in its implications of simultaneous life and death. But to my surprise, two other areas of the poem engage me even more, even though they essentially are bits of narrative, or stage-direction: "Beside that mountain road I hesitated" and "around our group I could hear the wilderness listen." In both these lines, the speaker is gathering himself at the threshold of his difficult decision, and I find myself caught up in the tautness of the moment. The whole poem, after all, is about striking a balance between two kinds of compassion, one tender and one dutiful; in the second passage, especially, the poem holds all its values in suspension, as in the moment before a judge renders a verdict. In this brief narrative, the end of the fourth stanza marks what would be identified in fiction as the crisis or turning point, after which the speaker's final gesture, dramatic as it is, nevertheless is part of that moment's outcome, or resolution.

To conclude, I offer one of my long-time favorites, an early poem by Adrienne Rich. Unlike the other poems we've examined, *The Loser* adheres strictly, albeit gracefully, to a fixed form: rhymed iambic tetrameter couplets within its six-line stanzas, and two distinct sections of equal length, each of which works as a complete poem on its own:

The Loser

> A man thinks of the woman he once loved; first,
> after her wedding, and then nearly a decade later.

> I kissed you, bride and lost, and went
> home from that bourgeois sacrament,
> your cheek still tasting cold upon
> my lips that gave you benison
> with all the swagger that they knew—
> as losers somehow learn to do.

> Your wedding made my eyes ache; soon
> the world would be worse off for one
> more golden apple dropped to ground
> without the least protesting sound,
> and you would windfall lie, and we
> forget your shimmer on the tree.

Beauty is always wasted: if
not Mignon's song sung to the deaf,
at all events to the unmoved.
A face like yours cannot be loved
long or seriously enough.
Almost, we seem to hold it off.

II

Well, you are tougher than I thought.
Now when the wash with ice hangs taut
this morning of St. Valentine,
I see you strip the squeaking line,
your body weighed against the load,
and all my groans can do no good.

Because you still are beautiful,
though squared and stiffened by the pull
of what nine windy years have done.
You have three daughters, lost a son.
I see all your intelligence
flung into that unwearied stance.

My envy is of no avail.
I turn my head and wish him well
who chafed your beauty into use
and lives forever in a house
lit by the friction of your mind.
You stagger in against the wind.[5]

I can never read those final lines without feeling a quiet welling of
joy. By then, this tribute has passed from an appreciation of the woman's
"shimmer on the tree," and the regret that her beauty is to be "wasted,"
to an acknowledgment of the seasoned, generative light of her "mind,"

which in this context includes her way of being, a beauty of character, that takes on a burnished quality against the grayness of that February day and the larger grayness of "nine windy years" of labor and loss. The final stanza evokes multiple layers of "friction," to use Rich's word, in its reference to the husband's having "chafed your beauty into use," and the gesture of "stagger[ing] in against the wind," as well as in the lovely image of "a house lit by the friction of your mind." All the tensions of the poem come into play in this final stanza—the pull of time, of weather, of labor, of marriage as a kind of erasure—only to highlight the enduring, magnified "shimmer" this woman now takes in the speaker's eyes. Certainly then, the final stanza is a viable center to the poem. And it is interesting to note that the form gets roughed up a bit in that stanza, the rhymes having turned to off-rhymes and thus creating subtle variation and tension in the poem's established music just where the content addresses tension through diction and image.

There are other points in this poem where off-rhyme occurs—the third and fourth lines of the first stanza, the first two lines of the second stanza, the whole third stanza, the last two lines of the fourth stanza, and the last two lines of the fifth stanza. Given Rich's obvious skill in choreographing the dance between form and content, I suggest that these areas indicate other hot spots in the poem which might be considered as smaller centers, or preparatory centers. The last two lines of the first section, for example, where "enough" and "off" create a particularly aggressive off-rhyme, provide the high-energy point of that section. "Mind" and "wind" do the same sort of work at the end of the second section. Variations of form often occur at "dark star" moments in formal poems such as Rich's, and investigation of these moments can add moisture to the dry discussions that sometimes ensue over fixed forms.

At this point I hope it is safe to observe that, ultimately, a poem's center does not always have to be relentlessly pursued and pinned down as long as the search has helped tune the reader in to the poem's greater and lesser frequencies. I often change my mind with the Rich poem, sometimes deciding on two centers and sometimes on one. Does that matter? The fact remains that "a dark star" has passed through me by the time I have finished reading this poem and that I am able, unlike the "you" in Tate's poem, to articulate and "share" the experience. While the Tate poem dazzled me by introducing the notion of "darkness" to the phenomenon of a star, Rich's poem leaves me warmed by the generative beauty of this woman who has been "squared and stiffened," who has lost her conventional "light" and now glows contrary to all expectation.

And I have that wonderful line, "a house lit by the friction of your mind," to keep in a corner of my own mind and pull forth like a talisman as I contemplate the possibilities of poetry as well as the possibilities of love. This, after all, is what lyric poems give us—brief enactments of a mind at work, acts of consciousness heightened by the impulse towards insight or revelation or equilibrium after some thought or event has "chafed" against it. The centers of poems bring us right up to those points of friction, and touching them allows us first to borrow, and then be filled with, their kindled light.

The essay above has focused on finding the centers in others' poems. I am less able to describe what it feels like to find a center in my own. But the following poem, I see in retrospect, makes an approach:

Secrets

Someone has vacated the premises,
the one who digs in the dark and comes back
with gold. The others mind the store
and have no truck with the mysteries

that breathe out there beyond
the straightforward fluorescents,
the predictable clock, the coins
exchanged for dry goods. I beseech

this someone for whom doors swing both
ways, on easy hinges, and whose intermittent
presence is more aura than conversation
but translates into word-strings lit

with travel: *Come home, come home, help me*
clear a path to the smoky fires and gypsy
songs, the questions that made me answer
in tongues. Come home and replenish the vein,

and sometimes a string of notes wafts
from beyond what the ear knows, or a scent
from a vanished world, or a scrap of memory
not mine that leads to a scene I can feel

and describe but don't—it's all
translation. My bones stretch, and then
dissolve. I reach for stars. For a time
I believe I can touch them.

TOWARDS A POETICS OF PULL-AND-RELEASE:
SOME THOUGHTS ON SILENCE IN POEMS

As artists, most of us have had to struggle first to make, then keep, a commitment to our originality and our quirky freedom, aspects of ourselves we cannot easily explain to loved ones or sell in the marketplace. We live in a culture that is dismissive and often hostile towards idiosyncrasy—at least more so now, during the early years of a new millennium, than in the early '70's, when many of us who teach allowed ourselves to become serious about writing. In those days, as a former magazine editor newly arrived at the University of Iowa Writers Workshop, I thought myself especially fortunate to be embarking on my journey at a time when, thanks to the innovations that had surfaced in late '50's and throughout the '60's, many kinds of expression seemed promising and viable, and the dynamics of experiential reading were explored with real passion.

In the past thirty-five years, I have watched the pendulum of taste swing to narrative poetry, to New Formalism, to Language poetry, to Deconstructionist poetry and other forms of the avant-garde, to the many ramifications of political correctness, to several resurgences of irony, and to different forms of self-consciousness or lack thereof. And without my quite being aware of it, the joy I originally experienced as a reader and writer of poetry has felt incidental at times, as if it had been edged aside by new values and voices; as a result, I sometimes have found myself hesitant to share it with others. I would not deny that ongoing attention to craft and technique, innovation that pushes us beyond our comfort level, and sensitivity to diverse cultures are vital to the discipline we have chosen. Nevertheless, I wish also to recall us to the aesthetic of openness of the early '70's, an aesthetic which I regard not as laziness on the reader's part or self-indulgence on the writer's part, but an actual discipline that requires a fair degree of athleticism of thought and feeling.

All of us, at times, bring ingrained habits to poems without meaning to. These habits can stem from a need to control, which arises by reflex in any situation where we feel threatened or uncertain or tired or distracted. Without warning we can feel imposed upon, then willful, and as a result we can become publicly or privately imposing. Many of my undergraduates were introduced to poetry by teachers who treated poems as codes to be unlocked rather than as mysteries to be solved at best partially, and often by indirection. Most of us who attended and now teach in writing programs have been in at least one workshop where the criticism seemed querulous, constricting. But as artists too, we know that when we impose and constrict in such ways, we put ourselves in opposition to otherness, hence to the flow of energy that can startle us into stepping beyond ourselves. We judge, and the judgment eventually works against our own freedom. Whether we are readers, teachers, poets or, as is often the case, all three, our alertness and a sense of adventure can be dampened by a preoccupation with performance or acceptance, or with proscribed kinds of clarity, in such a way as to pull a poem and its audience into an unconscious contest of wills.

I have in mind an alternative paradigm of control, one I've learned by becoming, well into my adulthood, a serious student of horsemanship. When a horse begins to break his concentration and accelerate his stride, the rider's tugging at the reins will only make the horse tug against the rider, whom he outweighs by more than a thousand pounds. But if the rider pulls briefly on the reins and releases them, pulls again and releases, she's engaging the horse in a different dynamic; she's getting his attention and then giving him a moment to respond. She's applying some degree of pressure and then backing off so he can make himself more comfortable by settling down. This method usually works if the rider stays patient and quiet and waits the moment out, and if the horse isn't too distracted by something else to yield his attention. He doesn't slow dramatically so much as steady himself, relax his stride, lower his head, and get on with the work at hand. In this paradigm, "control" becomes guidance by suggestion, and its impetus stems from intention tempered with restraint, as opposed to reflex and thoughtless will.

Pull and release. Pull again and release. It's more of a dance than a contest. It gives both parties a role. It gives the horse, who is not at the initiating end of intention, a chance to make some decisions of his own.

Silence, either within a poem itself or within the consciousness of a reader as she navigates a poem, is analogous to the invitation of a "release" as it facilitates a give-and-take relationship between reader and text. While silence is conventionally understood as restraint, it is also an aspect of rhythm, the down-swell that follows a decisive gesture made by language. It is like an intake of breath, without which the rhythm of breath's action, and the force of breath itself, would not be possible. Silence is often, but not always, white space. It is a moment created by the poem itself. Silence is easier to experience while reading a poem at one's own pace than while listening to one read aloud at someone else's pace. It is usually least detectable in a first reading and then richer, more conducive to real savoring, with subsequent readings.

Towards A Poetics Of Pull-And-Release: Some Thoughts On Silence in Poems

While a silence placed rightly in context can contain and communicate what is indescribable, unparaphrasable, and ultimately most meaningful about a poem, I wish nevertheless to be as specific as I can in identifying and illustrating the kinds of work silence can do. Here is a short poem which contains a central, pivotal silence that offers space for the reader to enter the poem. Such space is alive. It shimmers. It demands and then rewards the reader who is willing to meet it:

In Dispraise of Poetry

When the king of Siam disliked a courier,
he gave him a beautiful white elephant.
The miracle beast deserved such ritual,
that to care for it properly meant ruin.
Yet to care for it improperly was worse.
It appears the gift could not be refused.

—Jack Gilbert[1]

The silence in this poem dwells physically in the space between the title and the body of the poem, and it dwells tangibly in the friction between the abstractness of the title and the concreteness of the anecdote—between the fullness of the word, "poetry," and the more astringent, ironic bit of reportage which brings the title down to earth—to its senses, in a way, like a dose of smelling salts. The gap between title and text is the place where crucial implications flower, where the poet steps back, or "releases" the "pull" of the poem's two decisive gestures. The reader may not feel this dynamic very much or even at all during a first reading, but once she has the end of the poem to hold in mind, the title and space immediately following become electric. In Gilbert's piece, the title may well be the first half of the poem, and the text the second half. The reader can best feel the brunt of the poem's wit and implication when balanced right between the two, literally in the space that contains no words.

Here is a short poem by Mary Ruefle that uses silence even more subtly, certainly less physically than Gilbert's:

From Memory

The old poet riding on horseback in winter
came face to face with a thief who had
beaten his horse to a pulp. Once and for
all, they recognized each other without
speaking; one held a bright knife to the
other's throat while the other offered the
bleeding velvet of his animal to show that
he, too, had smuggled his life through
every conceivable hour.[2]

For me, the central silence in this poem is the phrase, "Once and for/all, they recognized each other without/speaking... ." Or perhaps more accurately, the central silence falls on either side of this statement, this moment, which arrives so smoothly in the flow of narrative yet forces the reader to pause, startled at the implication that the two startled figures have met before. This moment touches upon what the poem doesn't say, what the poem may have subtracted from itself in order to reach its provocatively pared-down state. And because the reader is never told what the poet and the thief "recognize" in each other, she is forced more deeply into the utterances the poem does make; in other words, she is forced not so much to "understand" the context of this phrase as to enter it and take it in like the air she breathes. Something very complex is being said here, and with disarming restraint. The astonishing moment of recognition equalizes these two archetypal figures, one the supposedly gentle poet and one the supposedly reprehensible thief. It brings them into an ambiance of metaphor without actually finishing the metaphor into an image, and without doing anything else to clarify or persuade. The two simply are held up as parallel concepts, and in that moment the reader is invited to make some effort, to push these archetypes even farther through an implicit sense of their differences, into some recognition of their similarities. True, the poem offers some help in its last two lines, but even this seemingly direct statement of how the two are similar is itself full of silence, and therefore of *implication.* Implication is a vital component of all good poems, whether or not they work by means of such compressed, active silences. To "smuggle [one's] life through every conceivable hour"—this is exhausting and thrilling to contemplate. "Every conceivable hour"—an "hour" becomes physical, like a mail slot or a tunnel or an international boundary. This brief passage offers a great deal to think about.

Like Gilbert's poem, this one taps something profound and indescribable about the nature of poetry and does so without exertion, without explanation. It is the reader who does the work of insight, having entered the space the poem clears within itself by raising a question, an opening in which a felt or implicit answer bubbles up from the text as well as from the reading/dreaming self who has come to the poem.

It is difficult for a poem to get away with making such demands on a reader, and with giving a reader so much freedom to roam, without falling apart. Ruefle's poem succeeds because each utterance it does make carries great weight and is instantly graspable, not to mention elegant. The two images it offers are lovely and surprising—"bright knife" and "bleeding velvet of his animal." They serve to ground the poem in a visualizable world that provides balance to the more philosophical dimensions the poem reaches for and attains. In addition, this poem is spoken line by line with quiet confidence. It allows the reader to feel guided even as she is provoked. In my own reading, I find myself inclined to trust it enough to settle in and do the work it asks, like the skittish horse whose rider keeps her own body quiet and makes intermittent, decisive gestures.

Now I offer a longer poem whose silences, though aided by the use of tercets and fairly short lines, nevertheless are not built into the poem itself as clearly as they are in Gilbert's and Ruefle's poems. Instead, Sandra McPherson's *On a Picture of My Parents Together in Second Grade* invites the attentive reader to create silences in her own mind—to pause voluntarily and often in order to savor the provocations offered by each of the poem's moments. Its speaker is un-groomed and unselfconscious, someone apparently not concerned with a need to elaborate upon, or craft transitions between, utterances which seem to come from the spontaneous formation of thought as it gropes its way through memory. The scene she depicts is rendered impressionistically so that the reader gets only a partial sketch of the literal elements that lead to the rich interiority of the experience even though it is occasioned by both a photograph and the occurrence of a minor accident. The poem's texture is quite different from the more cohesive, often more self-examining texture of a poem whose impetus comes from narrative or reflection. It contains holes but is not threadbare:

On a Picture of My Parents
Together in Second Grade

Dust as beige pongée,
'cot blossoms inside the margins,
  the palms with thin tigerstripes of blood and gravel...

But today, without a license, as I drive
a car black as the blind mules
in the old McPherson cinnabar mine,

it's for some foolish emergency
that I crash into the schoolyard,
into the fence that worried over everyone

both our generations knew.
This is the last time for me.
I will never go anywhere so quickly as into the past.

I wait but no one comes to help or accuse.
The square is full of devils
winding all free dust up into themselves. The accident

has spared each brick, electric bell, cursive letter, girl
in hula skirt and principal behind
the bricks, daydream

of lilac scent, violet
of iodine.
Anyone I might have hit,

their intelligence ordered here from madness of their parents'
bed to sit by surname and stand by height,
still belongs to tomorrow,

to the very green soap, salamander tank, and
zither which have always kept them wise
and curious.

A little mixing on the fingertips and my blood forms brothers,
the dust spins over the crosswalk,
I slam the door and follow the cloud home.

They will be glad I too am still together.[3]

This poem acts upon me as a string of stunning single moments, arrivals, which make me want to pause over each one even as they generate energy that helps the poem move forward and occasionally, surprisingly, circle back on itself by means of its gathering echoes. I pause often in this poem, each pause a voluntary moment of silence, and I experience each of them a little differently. The first pause is one of astonishment and pleasure at the image of the "car black as the blind mules/in the old McPherson cinnabar mine." "Black" and "blind" create an intense sense of blackness, especially in implicit relation to the underground world of the mine. Yet "cinnabar" warms this blackness, if one knows the deep coral color of this substance; if not, then the music of the word itself, like a single note from an exotic Middle Eastern instrument, may send a glowing thread through the blackness.

I pause again at the line, "into the fence that worried over everyone," because I feel the poem suddenly gathering itself towards a new dimension, away from the literal scene—now I can sense the *something more* that is at stake in the poem. And then, I inhabit a pleasurable sense of suspension over the stanza break to the arrival in the next line, "both our generations knew," where I suddenly feel the quiet force of the poem's confidence, its ease with dwelling in two realms at once. Now I have entered the poem's second realm, perhaps the realm that fueled the poem in the first place, the ambiance of family history.

I pause again soon after, at the line, "I will never go anywhere so quickly as into the past." This sentence, which takes on an arresting, unspoken physicality as a metaphor for the literal crash, pushes me even deeper into my felt sense of the poem's real subject, and then leaves me to my own devices while the next stanza returns to the literal scene and begins a section marked by lower intensity.

A few lines later, I experience several small pauses, like the syncopated bursts of light and color made by some fireworks, in the specific list of images behind the school's brick wall—the "single cursive letter, girl/in hula skirt" (Why a hula skirt? What exuberance might have led to its being worn?), the appealingly mixed sensations I get from the phrase, "violet of iodine," and so on. Each item in this list startles me, moves me beyond my expectations, reminds me that even in this linear section grounded in the literal scene, McPherson's poem wants to work fundamentally through the more holographic landscape of imagination and memory. In addition, it is boldly subjective in what it chooses to observe among the things it could have observed—names carved into desks, for instance, or chewing gum stuck to chair bottoms—and it draws the reader in to share in its boldness, its oddness.

I pause for different reasons in the middle of this list, in the entire stanza beginning with "their intelligence ordered here from madness of their parents'/bed to sit by surname and stand by height/still belongs to tomorrow... ." Here, I savor the elegance of the syntax, the tremendous amount of ground covered in all three lines, the pleasing rhythms and alliterations in the phrase, "sit by surname and stand by height." I love the flow of my attention—a physical sensation, a kind of dance—ordered by the line breaks in that stanza.

And finally, I pause at the notion that the objects in the schoolroom "have always kept" the children not just amused or informed, as one would expect, but "wise/and curious." The children are not just witnesses; these objects have given them a greater energy of curiosity, which they bring back to the objects in a continual dynamic of reciprocity. And they have been kept "wise" as well, kept in a state of alertness and transformation. Their relation to the schoolroom's objects feels similar to mine with this entire poem.

Thus, it is as a satisfied and well-exercised reader that I slip through the rest of the poem, whose energy diminishes towards the end but does so in such a way as to let me savor the layerings of nuance I've been given. By the time I reach the last line, I've caught up with the poem and am poised to share in the final little leap it makes. I do not feel the same breathlessness at the end of this poem that I've felt several times along the way; rather, I experience a welcome sense of comprehension that seems graceful and appropriate; my circuits have been charged but not overloaded.

Having identified as best I can my own experience as a reader of this poem, I am now in a position, as I shift from reader to teacher, to help an undergraduate literature class understand what it means as well as what it does, or to further examine it in a graduate-level workshop; in other words, I can now articulate its themes and sub-themes and the role played by sections I respond to less viscerally than the ones I've mentioned. Or I can question it. These issues apply to a less immediate, more cerebral, and perhaps to some readers or students a more useful level of response. But I maintain that our interaction with the silences in a well-made poem engage us in a preliminary intuitive connection with the impulses of the text and thus supply a crucial foundation for subsequent layers of response.

✒

Clearly, as the poems I've discussed reveal, silence in a poem often follows an image which resonates in the reader's consciousness, or a moment caught and frozen like a tableau. Silence often surrounds a moment in which the juxtaposition of two almost-but-not-quite-dissimilar images is experienced, the kind of leap Robert Bly talks about in his book, *Leaping Poetry*, a dynamic common in poems that draw energy from Surrealism.

I used to think only the image could generate energy, by itself and in conjunction with other images, like a stone thrown in a pond to create concentric rings; that is, I used to think the crucial point of energy was concreteness, the appeal to the senses and to our sense of being part of matter ourselves. But lately I've come to see that skillfully contexted *statements* can carve out space for themselves too, in the form of a reflective leap the mind makes, a slanted observation, a comment that goes a step or two ahead of the expected arrival, or an odd twist of thought. Statements work this way in poems by Louise Glück, William Stafford, Linda Gregg, and Jack Gilbert. A statement, like an image, can create a moment of paradox in a poem, or a place where two elements are seamlessly juxtaposed and reconciled.

And in the silence that follows, which is also a gesture in its implicit recognition of the importance of what has just been said, the reader becomes the active agent by invitation. The reader actually *does* something in a space or a silence; his or her thought moves beyond the stimulus to finish the thought, the moment, the gesture, and perhaps to recognize a starburst of implications. In a successful poem, the reader advances the thought of the poet like a relay runner accepting the baton. There's a rush of comprehension that can be felt instantly at many levels though not easily articulated. And it can occur several times along the way, not just at the end of a poem.

What I have just described is nothing new, either in critical theory or in terms of most readers' experience if they have read and enjoyed a fair amount of poetry. I would guess that most of us who write started doing so after we had experienced others' poems as though we had written them ourselves; we got to experience the high, the endorphins generated by someone else's exercise, and we were hooked. But I continue to be amazed at how easy it is for us to breathe bad faith into poems, our own and others', and how it often leads us to want to control them in accordance with some outside agenda. A reasonable amount of good faith may well be the opposite of control—good faith as acquiescence and the willingness to wait, even work, for gratification. Yet I'm also amazed at how little critical vocabulary there is for describing specific poems in terms of how the reader might acquiesce to them. Writers like William Stafford and Paul Carroll explored this area in the 1960's and '70's, but their voices have faded from the classroom and lecture hall. Robert Bly did too, in his essay, *What the Image Can Do*, where he described in detail the image as a conduit between the conscious and unconscious realms.

But the writer who has come closest to enacting the dynamics of participatory reading consistently in book after book, although he never would have called himself a literary critic, is the French philosopher of science I have mentioned, Gaston Bachelard, who embraced a phenomenological approach to literary works and articulately lost himself to the sensual and associative impact of not so much whole works as their individual moments. Colette Gaudin, one of his translators, describes him in the introduction to a compilation of selections from his many books, *On Poetic Imagination and Reverie*, as he might have described himself: "an avid reader, an advocate of leisurely and repeated reading."[4] Ecstatic yet precise, his responses to poetic passages bloom with references, images, and speculations that occur to him as he reads. His analytical writing is incandescent and admiring, enlivened by his trust in what he feels to be the poet's original "reverie" and in the reverie the poem consequently sparks in him, the reader.

Gaudin defines phenomenology, as Bachelard used it in his appreciation of literature, as "a description of the immediate relationship of phenomena with a particular consciousness... ."[5] In my discussion of McPherson's poem, I tried to follow this approach, using my reactions as a way to make objective observations about the poem as the initiator of those reactions. For Bachelard, Gaudin says, "...the best way to study images is to explore their power of trans-subjectivity. They *reverberate* in the reader's consciousness and lead him to create anew while communicating with the poet."[6]

Susan Sontag stresses in her essay, *On Style*, the dependence of a work of art "upon the cooperation of the person having the experience, for one may see what is 'said' but remain unmoved, either through dullness or distraction." She continues, "Art is seduction, not rape...art cannot seduce without the complicity of the experiencing subject."[7]

Complicity, then, is the key to how a reader and a poem might engage and finally transform one another. This alchemy is possible when will is absent (or nearly so) on both sides, and willingness, or faith, is aroused instead. Still, some poems invite this openness more than others. Many fine poems do not contain much silence, or space for a reader to step in and act. For obvious reasons, a more discursive or narrative poem will

Towards A Poetics Of Pull-And-Release: Some Thoughts On Silence in Poems

contain few or none of the jolts, leaps, and idiosyncrasies of the kind of poem I've been talking about.

※

In a workshop setting, this kind of poem, when it works, can provoke students and teachers alike to stretch their critical vocabulary as well as exercise their trust in their own instincts. Sontag suggests a whole new realm of terminology when she maintains that the ultimate aim and justification for a work of art is the "act of comprehension accompanied by voluptuousness." Bachelard uses words like "élan," "excess," and "exaltation" to describe responses certain images generate in him. It is difficult to find words for the deeply engaged, visionary states of mind, or the visceral sensations, which a poem may evoke. But we can be poets in the classroom as well as on the page; we can keep trying to approach with words what words fail to describe. And in the process we can learn to question ourselves briefly before we jump—here I borrow a phrase from a lecture by my Vermont College colleague Betsy Sholl—to "refine the surprises" from others' poems as well as our own. For me, it has helped to use terms like *felt logic, felt connections,* and *choreography,* which make at least modest room for idiosyncrasies in a poem, and for intuitive work on the part of the reader. In addition, some poems have *charisma, chutzpah,* a crazy sort of authority that can win us over.

Still, the kind of poem I've been talking about is exceptionally vulnerable, not only to being dismantled for wrong reasons but also to not working even on its own terms. There is only so much a willing reader can and should do. What techniques, then, and what kinds of attentiveness might we cultivate in order to write a poem that invites a reader into its explicit or implicit gaps and then rewards the effort?

Here are a few concrete suggestions about how to write a poem that skillfully uses silence:

Contexting of elements is of paramount importance; a writer can get away with putting anything in a poem if she sets up a context for it. Contexting has to do with the selection and ordering of images and observations, which I mentioned earlier, and it requires considerable patience. In this case the writer has to engage in complicity with her own poem. She must be willing to hear the "reverberations" of her own material independently of her intentions for that material, and then be willing to arrange and re-arrange and re-arrange again, until the piece achieves a flow that feels provocative and right, i.e., oddly logical, perhaps inexplicably so. And in the process she often must sacrifice passages that just don't carry their weight despite the role they may have had in making her believe in the poem in the first place. Conversely, she may find that a statement which at first seemed flat or rhetorical may become electric, compelling, in a context where it works in friction with another element or advances the poem beyond the expectations it seems to have set up, as we saw in Ruefle's and McPherson's poems.

I still see the *image* as essential to establishing immediacy and grounding a poem in a sense of place or motif or occasion, in addition to engaging the reader's senses in complex and pleasurable ways. Even a few well-envisioned and well-placed images can give a poem the kind of authority that allows it also to make statements or use abstractions without disintegrating into low-energy language. In other words, images can do much to set up a context that allows other moments in the poem to work successfully.

Recurrence, re-evocation of a central motif, is also a helpful device, especially as it gives cohesion to a poem that wants to move by means other than that of a mediating voice. The McPherson poem contains several references to generations, to ancestry, to the simultaneous existence of past and present, which repeatedly pull the reader not so much into a comprehension as into a *sensation* of her of family history as it centers around the schoolyard. It is my participation in this motif that makes me ultimately appreciate the resonance of her title. Then the references to dust devils, dust and blood on the hand, and dust on the crosswalk provide another pattern of repetition, so that the poem establishes a kind of material dialogue with itself, a pattern supple and open as a spider web. Recurrence can also take the form of repeated words, phrases, or lines— think of the unpolished and emotionally intense cohesion of some sestinas, pantoums, and villanelles.

And finally, *consulting others*. Especially with the kind of poem I'm talking about, it is important to consult readers whose judgment can be trusted, because it is important to hear one's poem through others' ears. If a poem is to invite complicity from the reader, its writer has to know where and how that invitation may be giving mixed signals.

I have used the word *intention* several times in this discussion, and I would like to conclude by focusing on it, especially as it accomplishes what more forceful *will* would accomplish but in a different way. To return to my paradigm of horse and rider, I picture a rider taking a horse over a pattern of jumps which requires a tight turn after each jump to set up the approach to the next. Novice riders are taught to look straight ahead while going over a jump, but on a more advanced course, the straight aim of the rider's gaze will cause her to make the turn too late and too wide for an effective approach to the next jump. Most of that turn will be spent in pulling on the reins, overcorrecting, and confusing the horse. However, if the rider goes over a jump with her head turned and her eyes focused on the next jump, the horse will land already canted into the turn, keeping his forward momentum and making a smooth track to his destination. To feel this difference on horseback is amazing; the first method requires a tremendous exertion of energy, is scary, and often doesn't work, while the second works so immediately it seems to bypass the muscles altogether in a kind of telepathic exchange. In the literal sense, the rider's turning her head engages balance rather than strength. The horse follows the direction of the rider's gaze because a chain reaction has been set up through the rider's body and consequently through his own.

Intention, for a poet's purposes, is like that of the rider visualizing the overall course well enough to anticipate mentally, hence physically, each next step. Intention, in other words, is an unarticulated but felt sense of direction which can ease us writers into acquiring a measure of the calmness, the grace under pressure that makes athletes perform well. It has to do with the visceral sense we bring to a poem, our intuitive link to its fledgling impulses, and our faith in the trajectory we feel as its potential even as we negotiate the demands of craft.

In essays, I'm attracted to the challenge of finding words for *felt* elements, like intention, which lose much of their resonance when one tries to analyze them too directly or lay down a formula for how to implement them. Nevertheless, a craft essay indeed is meant to illuminate such things sufficiently, at least by analogy if not a more direct approach, so that a writer or teacher might make personal use of them.

In poems, I allow myself to explore sensation without defining it at all. To walk around it and approach it diffusely. To use language in the service of pure evocation, which of course takes me beyond the originating sensation into others. I've chosen to add this poem—which happens to be a blank-verse sonnet whose title echoes one of Wright's most anthologized poems—because it offers an expression of how it feels to be in the presence of poems whose intentions invite trust and then—well, flight:

Reading James Wright on Flight 357 from Albuquerque to Chicago

Sometimes a poem offers a series of
chance encounters—partial phrases that slip
into the next seat and lift me before
I re-engage approved electronic
devices. Sometimes a poem reads my mind
in that private space before thought gathers
itself into subject/verb, cause/effect—
the shades are down but I can see in
or the words are clear and the spaces between them are shades closing off the whole sky
of what's been left out—a spare, thrilling diet.
When my feet touch cracked tarmac again, part
of me remains behind a high, golden
window. Sealed off from the thronged neon streets.

A MEDITATION ON PLACE, REAL AND IMAGINED

What, I wonder, do other poets hold or build in their minds as they draft a poem? Sound patterns? Rhythmic beats? A thread of narrative? I have come to realize that, for me, visualization is dominant; a whole landscape seems to take shape behind the material as I move a poem from a tentative to surer shape. More often than not the landscape is an imaginary one—a tandem, effortless invention that rarely becomes part of the poem itself. Faulty as my memory is when it comes to things like book titles, quotations, and even my own lines, I can call back the landscape that backlit every poem I have ever written; this includes poems that have little or no actual landscape, as well as poems built around voices and experience not my own. I find myself inhabiting a kind of stage set, a backdrop, a tapestry that gathers depth and color and feeds the poem in inexplicable ways. Like dreams, these backdrops can be hard to describe, the placement of their elements suffused with mood or atmosphere that gives cohesion to what might otherwise come across as random detail. In the case of *Before They Plowed the Orchard Under,* however, the backdrop bloomed real and ready-made, a loved landscape generating layers of attendant memory, from which I could pluck a few details like apples the speaker plucks off the trees in the poem.

For many years, during the bulk of my career as a professor and writing program director at University of Texas-El Paso, I lived in a rented house—a little jewel of a house—on a 160-acre farm in the Rio Grande valley just over the state line in Southern New Mexico. I and my neighbors kept horses there, and at times four Longhorn cows and a few llamas shared tenancy as well. Behind us rose the Chihuahuan desert, all sand, mesquite and creosote, to mesas we could reach easily on horseback. Below us lay fields of alfalfa and cotton that stretched the five-mile width of the valley to the Rio Grande, and beyond that lay the long silhouette of the Franklin Mountains. Pecans and apples grew on the property as well, though indeed the main orchard, which was re-graded every year by tractors using laser equipment, eventually was sold to someone who lost the funds to maintain it. Living on this acreage, in a house full of windows and with the constant presence of one, sometimes two horses that needed daily care and almost daily exercise, opened windows in me through which the light and landscape of the place flowed easily.

I remember, but retain, little *visceral* memory, of the many mornings I woke up anxious and propelled to action by the pressures of teaching, or of the long hours of committee work at school and grading at home. I am rarely re-visited by the more unsettling moments of schooling and suppling an antsy Thoroughbred mare that never should have been put on a race track at the age of two and whose wild eyes finally softened five years after I had taken her out of training and given her a less demanding life under my sole care. What dwells instead, and now grows in my memory, is the wash of fresh, exhilarating light I stepped into every morning as I went out to feed horses and clean their pen, and the soft call-and-response of quail rummaging nearby, and the panorama of sand, fields, and mountains that never failed to settle me for the day ahead, reminding me I lived cupped in something vast and benevolent. I took all this in whenever I looked out of any window of my house on my way from one preoccupation to another. I took it in as I groomed a horse and cleaned tack after a long, dusty ride.

I took it in every time I came back to the farm from central El Paso, that other universe, and felt the deepening light, another shade of benevolence, settle around me once again.

So yes, the smell of those fermenting apples in the poem is emblematic of my daily returns to that world, just as the apple blossoms offer a fractional glimpse of the rhythms of the seasons that transformed the light, colors and scents of the land and transformed *me* in ways I am still coming to understand. The memory of the warm, sunlit apples Nicky and I shared on our return from the schooling field or open desert still makes me also taste that restful sense of being-in-the-moment following our bouts of focused, physical work. It makes me recall the calm pleasure I felt in my surroundings whenever I stepped off my own racetrack mind and looked around me. In this brief essay, I have written more than I ever have about a vast Southern New Mexico land that for many years held me and was my home. It never ceased being a novelty to me, a person raised in the Midwest. I would never try or even want to write a poem explicitly about this special place, but now and then small, elliptical bits of it take me by surprise and find their way into poems like the one about an orchard that no longer exists:

———————————————

A Meditation On Place, Real And Imagined

57

Before They Plowed the Orchard Under

Every fall the branches were jeweled with
warm, fist-sized apples we could pick from horseback
though we lived in the desert, which may explain
the barely perceptible sweetness of their flesh.
Nicky ate hers out of my hand, each apple in two neat bites.

Late autumn into winter, the whole ranch smelled
of windfalls and sun, amber fermenting
and seeping into the sand as though into a tavern's
old wood floor—I felt giddy each time I drove home
through the early dusk, rolling down my window

though it wouldn't be until spring, when the river
filled the ditches and the trees released a froth of white
and pink against the grey mountains, that their own
celebration, saved for the new season, made them
sway all night in their plumage, their drinking songs.

Here are two poems that served me as different approaches to writing about place: one from the perspective of a visitor whose perceptions are sharpened as she feels herself diminished yet imaginatively provoked by the foreignness of the setting, and the second from the perspective of pure imagination:

Venezia Notturno

Liquid streets. Their shimmer—
the space between Petrarch's first line
and the sonnets he left in his wake—

pathways between houses where I
feel my way out of my neon century
to a bridge barely visible in the damp

arrival of dusk. I would borrow a sliver
of lamplight edging from high shutters—
I would borrow a whole slice of

someone's evening after he has closed
his shop full of yellow ceramics
and poured red wine into a tumbler,

spreading the day's news by his plate
and leaving his shutters open
as the mist he's used to

settles like a hush, caesura
in the metrics of history which only seem
to pause at the present—a trick offered

to visitors from my country, where no one
has ever carried groceries over
cobblestones softened by hooves and blood

or lived in a city where houses rise
right from the water, their foundations
part salt, part tidal drift.

In Venezia, a single gondola glides
now and then through the sleep of those
who were born to the sound of sealed wood

parting water, the near-silence from which
the gilt and filigree of the Renaissance rose
like hothouse vegetation to become cathedral

and palace, each piazza a fugue
of torso and limb, gilt wings of cherubs,
marble carved to a froth, busy frescoes

climbing the Doge's walls one frame at a time—
thus the metropolis of ceilings
came to be, a painter secured by ropes

suspended beneath each one, his palette full of gold
and a blue that was even harder to come by
while the lagoon continued its slow art
below, even at night, stroking stone to silt.

The Story I Need

After a line by Ricardo Molinari

Ah, if only the village were so small
and I could look into others' windows by
looking into my own cupped hands

to see what steams on their
plates, or read the spines of books
on their shelves, all those lives

to open one at a time, I might hold
the history of civilization a little closer
to my own small history—bread
passed down from the centuries, leather boots
on flagstone, couples' first words

in the morning—not for the privacies
but as proof of the way buildings hold the countless
small movements of words and bodies
through space, and for the feeling

that I, too, am drying the cups and putting them away
or sitting at the tavern, a chessboard
open between me and the oldest inhabitant

or joining a family at their picnic on the green,
unable to distinguish myself from
the murmuring parents and noisy siblings
gathered around the cheese and pears
they have chosen, in a world

of possibilities, to set on the bright cloth.

THE "PERSONAL" POEM AS SACRED SPACE

*P*oets have conceived their poems from personal, deeply interior spaces throughout the ages, as in most of the poetry defined as *lyric*. Yet the word *personal* has become a minefield in the realm of contemporary critical discourse, linked as it is with the Confessional movement of the 1960's, whose impulses were originally liberating but now, in many respects, appear tiresome. The refined bravery of Lowell and Snodgrass, and the more explosive revelations of Plath, Berryman, Sexton, and Ginsberg, drove a wedge against the formal distancing, the taste for orderly surfaces that had reigned over American poetry all the way through the 1950's despite the influence of Whitman and Williams. The work of these first Confessional poets gave subsequent generations of writers permission to *not* disguise the self, to *not* mute strong feeling, and thus to put a great deal of newly available energy into exploring the self as a legitimate frontier. Their work also helped set the stage for explorations of organic form, the subconscious, and untapped aspects of uniquely American life and landscape, all of which characterized much of the poetry written throughout the 1960's and remain the legacy of that decade. Understandably, however, the landscape of self the Confessional poets illuminated with liberating candor is no longer a frontier at all in a culture that since then has come to embrace psychotherapy, recovery groups, talk shows and, in its literature, the memoir as a literary genre.

In recent years, poets who write lyric poetry using the undisguised "I" often have been accused of being overly "sincere" about their feelings and, thus, to borrow from Alicia Ostriker's summary of critics' pre-1960's response to much poetry written by women, their poems "[are] dismissed as self-absorbed, private, escapist, non-universal... ."[1] Sincerist poetry is said to jettison craft, irony, subtleties of tone, and the visionary capabilities of imagination in favor of a transcription of autobiographical elements that more often than not feature a wounded self. Some of these observations are well-taken, but like any other reaction to a status quo, they can become dogma in and of themselves—reductive, patronizing, and restrictive, especially to young writers whose need for approval can steer them away from valid experiments.

To anyone with a taste for the "personal" in poems, it seems more important than ever to seek models in writers who offer, along with glimpses into their lives and inner landscapes, provocative restraint and selectivity in their handling of detail and also a less definable quality, insight distilled anew in poem after poem. For me, the personal poetry of Linda Pastan, Jack Gilbert, Jane Kenyon, and William Stafford has these qualities to such a degree that it defies labels and the waxing and waning of controversies. Their poems soar beyond the singular life but remain connected to it, like kites in a good wind. Theirs is the sort of poetry I find myself turning to first thing in the morning, before the day's obligations take the edge off my alertness, so that I might absorb some of the calm and clarity of their inner lives and the resultant sense of entering some—dare I say it?—inviolate personal space along with the speaker. Their poems seem to arise from the self as sanctuary so purely that they replicate the experience of *being* in sanctuary; in this respect their poems bind poet, poem, and reader in a moment as intimate and transcendent as the act of prayer.

Such poems are not mired in the self but do seem to arise from an accessible life—from events, memories, and moments of feeling which appear to be neither disguised nor exploited. Such poems are acts of meditation more than they are confessions. They may refer to suffering but in the moment of their utterance have claimed breathing space from that suffering, are curiously at rest. Emotion recollected in tranquility is, of course, nothing new, but as the world changes, so do the pace and tenor of our language, and so do the selection and arrangement of perceptions and reflections to achieve and enact a still point. Indeed, the very nature of "recollection" and "tranquility" changes. Although Wordsworth is a fine exemplar of a poet who creates moments of sanctuary, his poems speak more formally and more neatly than we, in the cacophonous first quarter of a new century, speak to ourselves when we're surprised by insight or strong feeling that seems to derive its authority from something beyond the self. The work I'm about to discuss seems less conscious of itself as stronghold, or point of arrival. It renders intensely personal insights for the most part by means of an unspoken, redeeming humility, a willingness simply to bear witness and settle into a certain degree of irresolution rather than a need to clarify or conclude. As a result, the self reverberates in the work of these writers as a conduit rather than a locale.

As effortless or spontaneous as these poems appear to be, their authors do employ identifiable strategies of technique and perception. They also reveal attitudes and values which allow us to understand how they manage to locate themselves in an inviolate personal space and to not be more than intermittently overcome by the noise of the world. In terms of specific strategies, the work by these four differs in significant ways, but their poems offer in common a certain restraint of both tone and topography, often sustaining considerable white space (i.e., silence) within or around themselves; a sense of stillness from which emerge heightened powers of insight and observation; a grounding in the rhythms and laws of nature; and the sensation of a significant arrival, an opening from the cen-

The "Personal" Poem
As Sacred Space

65

ter, being achieved at the moment of writing. Suffering is not the subject of these poems, but one often has the impression they provide, for the writer, purchase against a potentially paralyzing despair; in this regard they move energy away from a suffering self, leaving a *sensate* self.

❧

Linda Pastan, the first of these poets, is probably the most vulnerable to attack by those who would dismiss undisguised treatment of domestic and family life, and an "I" firmly positioned in it, as worthy subjects. Like Emily Dickinson, Pastan presents herself as a visionary recluse, supremely aware of the forces that at once govern and extend far beyond her small realm and also beyond the apparently larger realm where history, for what it's worth, is made and taken seriously in its ever-repetitive chapters. "My house is my only heaven," she writes in *Self Portrait.* "As for my country, it blunders along/as well intentioned as Eve choosing/cider and windfalls, oblivious/to the famine soon to come./I stir pots, bury my face in books, or hold/a telephone to my ear as if its cord/were the umbilicus of the world/whose voices still whisper to me/even after they have left/their bodies."[2]

The following poem further illustrates the seemingly confined, yet expansive, quality of Pastan's powers of observation as they focus on what is immediately observable from her realm and then travel swiftly to greater mystery beyond:

Snowstorm

Just watching is enough,
as if the eyes were two headlamps,
the body a stalled vehicle
in all this whiteness:
the world embracing
the solidity of nothing at all,
filling every space
with a silence of pure
geometry—a galaxy
of crystals spinning
out of control. Until

in a blink, the clouds
part, the fuse
of the sun ignites a passion
of melting, a roar

down the rooftiles,
and here comes the world
as it was, untransformed,
ordinary, and I am
at the window, full
of a cold knowledge
I hardly understand.[3]

Pastan writes a poetry that is elegiac, stoic, and often oddly consoling in its perceptions of the ambushes and ambivalences of family life, the losses that accrue as generations pass and, most interestingly, the holographic nature of the most commonplace moment. For Pastan, the still center from which her poems arise is an awareness of the circular nature of time, the cycles that churn us into their vast machinery and pause but briefly on the fulcrum of the present. She writes in the poem *Balance:*

On the small, imaginary
kitchen scales,
I place on one side...
my mother's suede glove—
that emptied udder;

on the other the mitten
my grandson just dropped—
a woolen signpost he'll soon outgrow...
Equilibrium is simply
that moment when the present
is as real as the past
or the future... .[4]

Here is another example of Pastan's remarkable stillness as witness at the center of swirling, circular family history, and of the unassuming but unmistakable flash of wisdom that marks her arrivals:

The Laws of Primogeniture

My grandson has my father's mouth
with its salty sayings
and my grandfather's crooked ear
which heard the soldiers coming.

He has the pale eyes of the Cossack
who saw my great-great-grandmother
in the woods, then wouldn't stop
looking.

And see him now, pushing
his bright red firetruck towards
a future he thinks he's inventing
all by himself.[5]

The realm of family becomes, in Pastan's poetry, as profound a testing ground as any frontier or battlefield, and it is one she embraces even as she confronts its dangers. As she says in *Who Is It Accuses Us?*:

> Who is it accuses us of safety,
> as if the family were soldiers
> instead of hostages... .
> Consider the pale necks of the children
> under their colored head scarves,
> the skin around the husbands' eyes flayed
> by guilt and promises.
> You who risk no more than your own skins
> I tell you household gods
> are jealous gods...
> they will poison your secret wells
> with longing.[6]

Pastan is rueful and self-effacing in most of her poems, yet she speaks with authority that is no more lost on her than it is on us, grounded as she is in a domesticity that enacts nothing less than natural law—that is as much tenor as it is vehicle in any possible metaphor for human endeavor. And although she might have liked at least to have been "one of the Sirens" to her husband who returns "a little angry" from the world each evening, as she describes him in *You Are Odysseus,* she does not dismiss herself as a plainer Penelope, but acknowledges her perspective as particularly enduring as it arises from her position outside the male world of quest, conquest, and the making of what she sees as a limited version of history. At the end of the poem, she writes, "Meanwhile the old wars/go on, their dim music/can be heard even at night./You leave each morning,/soon our son will follow./Only my weaving is real."[7]

Like Linda Pastan, Jack Gilbert values isolation, having chosen to live for long periods of time in remote parts of Greece or New England, without running water or electricity, in a manner which scarcely seems touched by the twentieth century. His poems are suffused with this privacy, "[a] stillness so complete, you hear/the whispering inside you," as he describes it in the poem, *Betrothed*.[8] Understandably, his connections to weather and light, to the food his garden offers, to firewood, to water drawn from a well—in short, to the cycles and rituals of ordinary survival—ground his metaphysical life as they do his physical one. Within the asceticism of such a life, he confronts on many levels the tensions between desire and limitation, the sacred and the profane, and paradoxically he finds a still point for himself by dwelling fully within them:

Going Wrong

The fish are dreadful. They are brought up
the mountain in the dawn most days, beautiful
and alien and cold from night under the sea,
the grand rooms fading from their flat eyes.
Soft machinery of the dark, the man thinks,
washing them. "What can you know of my machinery!"
demands the Lord. *Sure,* the man says quietly
and cuts into them, laying back the dozen struts,
getting into the muck of something terrible.
The Lord insists: "You are the one who chooses
to live this way. I build cities where things
are human. I make Tuscany and you go to live
with rock and silence." The man washes away
the blood and arranges the fish on a big plate.
Starts the onions in the hot olive oil and puts
in peppers. "You have lived all year without women."

He takes out everything and puts in the fish.
"No one knows where you are. People forget you.
You are vain and stubborn." The man slices
tomatoes and lemons. Takes out the fish
and scrambles eggs. *I am not stubborn,* he thinks,
laying all of it on the table in the courtyard
full of early sun, shadows of swallows flying
on the food. *Not stubborn, just greedy.*[9]

Gilbert views the outside world as an impediment to authentic living—in his case as so much grinding of gears, posturings and power games, repetitive motion disguised as progress. He conveys this in one of my favorite poems, in which he evokes through powerful images the industrial life of his native Pittsburgh and then turns away, seeking his version of sanctuary:

Measuring the Tyger

Barrels of chains. Sides of beef stacked in vans.
Water buffalo dragging logs of teak in the river mud
outside Mandalay. Pantocrater in the Byzantium dome.
The mammoth overhead crane bringing slabs of steel
through the dingy light and roar to the giant shear
that cuts the adamantine three-quarter-inch plates
and they flop down. The weight of the mind fractures
the girders and piers of the spirit, spilling out
the heart's melt. Incandescent ingots big as cars
trundling out of titanic mills, red slag scaling off
the brighter metal in the dark. The Monongahela River
below, night's sheen on its belly. Silence except
for the machinery clanging deeper in us. You will
love again, people say. Give it time. Me with time
running out. Day after day of the everyday.
What they call real life, made of eighth-inch gauge.

Newness strutting around as if it were significant.
Irony, neatness and rhyme pretending to be poetry.
I want to go back to that time after Michiko's death
when I cried every day among the trees. To the real.
To the magnitude of pain, of being that much alive.[10]

For Gilbert, as for all these poets, real feeling signifies redemption,
life rightly lived. It blooms from the simplicity of silence and consequent
self-communion, whether or not the subject is the self. It is rendered
through language that embodies that silence and self-communion, and in
Gilbert's case this can be seen in the pacing and exquisite selectivity of his
images, observations, and sentence fragments, each of which claims its
own space as an aphoristic moment within the poem. Gilbert is a particularly reticent yet intense poet; each image, each fragment, seems strained
through a grid work of memory and rigorous contemplation, all dross
removed, as the following poem illustrates:

Recovering Amid the Farms

Every morning the sad girl brings her three sheep
and two lambs laggardly to the top of the valley,
past my stone hut and onto the mountain to graze.
She turned twelve last year and it was legal
for the father to take her out of school. She knows
her life is over. The sadness makes her fine,
makes me happy. Her old red sweater makes
the whole valley ring, makes my solitude gleam.
I watch from hiding for her sake. Knowing I am
there is hard on her, but it is the focus of her days.
She always looks down or looks away as she passes
in the evening. Except sometimes when, just before
going out of sight behind the distant canebrake,
she looks quickly back. It is too far for me to see,
but there is a moment of white if she turns her face.[11]

So far, everything I have said about the poetry of "sacred space" applies equally to men and women. But there is one more aspect of Gilbert's work which fascinates me as a valid element of self-communion which I rarely see women writers in our culture inclined or able to do. On occasion he talks to God, "man to man," and seems to experience God at least some of the time as a not-unsympathetic friend: "The Lord sits with me out in front watching/a sweet darkness begin in the fields./We try to decide whether I am lonely," he says at the beginning of *The Lord Sits with Me out in Front*. He concludes, "He asks for the Brahms./We watch the sea fade. The tape finishes again/and we sit on. Unable to find words."[12] For Gilbert, God remains a traditional deity who neither oppresses nor consoles, who is in effect an equal. His poem, *Going Wrong*, quoted earlier, shows God engaging him in friendly argument. This collegial relationship to a supreme being puts Gilbert in a state of freedom that is, to use a word he would never use, dizzying.

For all his renunciations, Gilbert seems to see himself as part of the fabric of Western civilization. He quarrels or communes with a Judeo-Christian god. He writes of women as archetypally compelling and elusive, projecting on them a Grail-like mystery which can be seductive even as it is somewhat exploitative. He often speaks through the personae of romantic literary figures such as Don Giovanni, Prospero, and Dante. Indeed, much of the authority of Gilbert's work seems grounded in a conviction that his experiences as a man, even his renunciations, are representative ones—that his freedom to embrace or renounce comes from his birthright as product and inheritor of the classical world, an Arthurian world of heroic, if doomed passions. The very tone of his poems, ascetic and hard-edged, which lifts them beyond the dangers of unadorned confessionalism, seems to arise from a quiet but aggressive belief in the universality of the sacred space he has claimed for the self, as this poem reveals:

The "Personal" Poem
As Sacred Space

It thrashes in the oaks and soughs in the elms.
Catches on innocence and soon dismantles that.
Sends children bewildered into life. Childhood
ends and is not buried. The young men ride out
and fall off, the horses wandering away. They get
on boats, are carried downstream, discover maidens.
They marry them without meaning to, meaning no harm,
the language beyond them. So everything ends.
Divorce gets them nowhere. They drift away from
the ruined women without noticing. See birds
high up and follow. "Out of earshot," they think,
puzzled by *earshot*. History driving them forward,
making a noise like the wind in maples, of women
in their dresses. It stings their hearts finally.
It wakes them up, baffled in the middle of their lives
on a small bare island, the sea blue and empty,
the days stretching all the way to the horizon.[13]

Of all these poets, the one whose work most calls to mind the classical grace, the range of perception, and the unassuming spirituality of Wordsworth is Jane Kenyon. The self in her poems is no less firmly grounded in its moments of communion than is Gilbert's; nevertheless, it positions itself as more of a witness even in its acts of participation—a gracious witness, sometimes one quietly in need of consolation, whose impulse is to honor the subtle and enduring harmonies in what she observes. Perhaps another way to say this is that the self in her poems is oddly permeable, generous, almost transparent, not an epicenter the way Gilbert's is. Nor does she speak from an overt awareness of women's wisdom as distinct from men's, as Pastan does, although both women derive strength from, and identify with, cycles of nature, as more female than male poets have tended to do. In addition, Kenyon often finds her bearings in the contemplation of hers or her husband's ancestors who have left behind a recipe or tablecloth or thimble, and whose portraits keep the past alive within the walls of their old farmhouse. The speaker in her poems is fluid and responsive, sometimes consoled and sometimes quietly exultant to recognize herself as part of a continuum.

Kenyon's apparent lack of attitudes and agendas, coupled with the sheer exquisiteness of her poems, makes her work particularly hard to talk about. Her poems usually start with an immediate moment and locale and then travel great distances without seeming to, partly because they never leave the immediate world behind but instead deftly add layers to it. To say that unlike Gilbert she presents herself mostly as a witness is true but a bit reductive, as it risks overlooking the way her reflections enlarge the perceiving self and in effect link witnessing with the *action* of honing and strengthening the spirit, the soul, the capacious observer, whatever it is in all of us that yearns for sacred space. Note the range of her attention as it unfolds in the following poem:

The Guest

I had opened the draft on the stove
and my head was tending downward when
a portly housefly dropped on the page
in front of me. Confused by the woodstove's
heat, the fly, waking ill-tempered, lay
on its back, flailing its legs and wings.

Then it lurched into the paper clips.
The morning passed, and I forgot about
my guest, except when the buzz rose
and quieted, rose and quieted—tires
spinning on ice, chain saw far away,
someone carrying on alone... .[14]

*The "Personal" Poem
As Sacred Space*

The Guest illustrates how Kenyon manages, like Pastan, to see the world in a grain of sand, as she confines herself to a seemingly limited realm and then transcends it (but does not abandon it) suddenly at the end. The next poem journeys much farther both inward and outward, its apparent communion with nature complicated and darkened by an event that has preceded it. The event is referred to only briefly, more than halfway through the poem, in two abrupt lines of flashback, but it reverberates with other references which suggest trouble beneath the surface of her observations. Like many of Kenyon's longer poems, this one quietly covers a great deal of ground, organizing its observations around a dialogue in which nothing is resolved but a relationship is articulately, and even soothingly revealed between the enduring natural landscape and the troubled human one:

Frost Flowers

Sap withdraws from the upper reaches
of maples; the squirrel digs deeper
and deeper in the moss
to bury the acorns that fall
all around, distracting him.

I'm out here in the dusk,
tired from teaching and a little drunk,
where the wild asters, last blossoms
of the season, straggle uphill.
Frost flowers, I've heard them called.
The white ones have yellow centers
at first: later they darken
to a rosy copper. They're mostly done.
Then the blue ones come on. It's blue
all around me now, though the color
has gone with the sun.

My sarcasm wounded a student today.
Afterward I heard him running down the stairs.

There is no one at home but me—
and I'm not at home; I'm up here on the hill,
looking at the dark windows below.
Let them be dark. Some large bird
calls down-mountain—a cry
astonishingly loud, distressing.

I was cruel to him: it is a bitter thing.
The air is damp and cold,
and by now I am a little hungry... .
The squirrel is high in the oak,
gone to his nest, and night has silenced
the last loud rupture of the calm.[15]

Kenyon's poems squarely face the vicissitudes of inner weather, some quite dark, as when she writes of the depressions that plagued her throughout her life and the lingering illness that ended it while she was still in her forties. But they also reflect a celebratory spirit well nourished by connubial love, by tending and observing the natural world surrounding her home, and by her devotion to poetry. One can feel "sacred space" as a glowing presence in all her poems—a quiet joy in the very act of witnessing and retrieval, as can be seen in the following poem—and it is easy to imagine that Kenyon was as grounded by her acts of reflection as are we, her readers:

A Boy Goes Into the World

My brother rode off on his bike
into the summer afternoon, but
Mother called me back
from the end of the sandy drive:
"It's different for girls."

He'd be gone for hours, come back
with things: a cocoon, gray-brown
and papery around a stick;
a puff ball, ripe, wrinkled,
and exuding spores; owl pellets—
bits of undigested bone and fur;
and pieces of moss that might
have made toupees for preposterous
green men, but went instead
into a wide-necked jar for a terrarium.
He mounted his plunder on poster
board, gluing and naming
each piece. He has long since
forgotten those days and things, but
I at last can claim them as my own.[16]

The reader often finds him or herself dwelling solidly within a
Kenyon poem without having been aware of stepping over a threshold or
showing a passport. Her poems allow the reader immediate access to the
realm of the universal, via a line of feeling pure and true as a harmonic—a
soft but soaring vibration—from which arise her apt, startling observations.

William Stafford's work, in contrast, is propelled by agendas—benevolent ones—as he seeks again and again to instruct himself as well as his reader on the importance of keeping consciousness, memory, and conscience honed in a world that would blunt them: "…let me live definite, shock by shock," he asserts at the end of *At the Chairman's Housewarming*, in which he likens small talk to "jellyfish" that "coated the silver tine by tine,/folding meek spoons and the true knifeblades/and rolling a tentacle into the wine."[17] The most prolific of these four writers, with some three thousand poems in print, Stafford clearly experienced his writing as ongoing sacrament, daily meditation. A great number of his poems leave the impression of a speaker moving from one layer of consciousness to the next like a swimmer sometimes diving to unforeseen depths, sometimes surfacing clean and fresh from the waves.

The speaker of Stafford's poems often has a cagey naiveté, like Peter Falk's Columbo meandering and shuffling his way to the heart of things (more on him in a later essay). The naiveté is genuine in the sense that Stafford, like the other poets under discussion, seeks to remain apart from the materialistic and political world, although in his case outright ignorance of that world becomes the operative strategy. His observations often have the gentle, untainted directness of a child or an *idiot savant,* as can be seen in this poem:

Lit Instructor

Day after day up there beating my wings
with all of the softness truth requires
I feel them shrug whenever I pause:
They class my voice among tentative things.

And they credit fact, force, battering.
I dance my way toward the family of knowing,
embracing stray error as a long-lost boy
and bringing him home with my fluttering.

Every quick feather asserts a just claim;
it bites like a saw into white pine.
I communicate right; but explain to the dean—
well, Right has a long and intricate name.

And the saying of it is a lonely thing.[18]

As is evident in the following poem, Stafford's strategic guileless-ness was sometimes interpreted by critics as "simplicity," attracting the sort of censure that today would fall into the anti-sincerest mode. As is also evident, however, Stafford was not easily dislodged from the sanctuary of his own sensibility, and he even managed to feel curiously confirmed by the "truth" his critics offered up to him:

I wanted the plums, but I waited.
The sun went down. The fire
went out. With no lights on
I waited. From the night again—
those words: how stupid I was.
And I closed my eyes to listen.
The words all sank down, deep
and rich. I felt their truth
and began to live them. They were mine
to enjoy. Who but a friend
could give so sternly what the sky
feels for everyone but few learn to
cherish? In the dark with the truth
I began the sentence of my life
and found it so simple there was no way
back into qualifying my thoughts
with irony or anything like that.
I went to the fridge and opened it—
sure enough the light was on.
I reached in and got the plums.[19]

Stafford also seeks in many of his poems to retrieve what has been forgotten or overlooked—by himself as well as others. "I haven't told this before," he says at the beginning of *Something That Happens Right Now*,[20] and in a sense most of his poems convey that sense of bringing into the light and air of a one-on-one exchange a secret or a bit of buried treasure, be it a long-forgotten schoolmate who had to leave school early every day to cook for her father, a small-town librarian who quietly died of cancer decades ago, or the sudden memory of passing a hermit's island with a group of boyhood friends and for a moment feeling himself *become* the dweller of that distant hut.

The self in Stafford's poems taps into sacred space by fusing with the objects of his attention, especially when they exist within or represent the natural world. Again and again his poems enact a deeply instinctive reciprocity between self and other, and the self emerges from the interchange enlarged, blessed, as the possessor of a "gift." The following poem illustrates the porousness of Stafford's sensibility, and in addition, it offers in its last three lines a partial *ars poetica* on how he accesses and nurtures his own sacred space:

A Little Gift

Fur came near, night inside it,
four legs at a time, when the circus
walked off the train. From cage to cage
we carried night back to the cats and poured
it into their eyes, from ours. They
lapped steadily, and the sponge of their feet
swelled into the ground. Even today
I keep that gift: I let any next thing fold
quietly into the blackness that leads
all the way inward from the hole in my eye.[21]

Although Stafford has as masterful a touch as any of these poets with the apt and startling image, extended metaphor, and subtle applications of sound, his poems also contain outright statements, most of which seem to arise as revelations from the very act of writing, like the one that ends *A Little Gift*, although sometimes they provide entry to a poem which then carries or deepens them to further implications. "If you don't know the kind of person I am/and I don't know the kind of person you are/a pattern that others made may prevail in the world/and following the wrong god home we may miss our star," he says with frank didacticism at the beginning of *A Ritual to Read to Each Other*, which enjoins us to remain vigilant against our projections, "the horrible errors of childhood" that can distort our view of others and cause us to break our connections with "the parade of mutual life."[22] But perhaps because of his skill with the image, which gives his voice a concreteness that is also visionary, most of Stafford's poems manage not to founder in didacticism even though they clearly, if humbly, seek to gather us into their fold—to tell as well as show us how to preserve the life within ourselves by way of preserving the life all around us. This is a tall order, but one he embraces with conviction, often humor, and a vital component of restraint which allows him to create provocative spaces within his weavings of images and statements, and to know when an image is doing sufficient work on its own. His poem, *At the Bomb Testing Site*, stands one of one of the finest poems to emerge from the Protest Movement that flourished in the 1960's, partly because it focuses on a peripheral image rather than on obvious references to a nuclear explosion:

At the Bomb Testing Site

At noon in the desert a panting lizard
waited for history, its elbows tense,
watching the curve of a particular road
as if something might happen.

It was looking at something farther off
than people could see, an important scene

acted in stone for little selves
at the flute end of consequences.

There was just a continent without much on it
under a sky that never cared less.
Ready for a change, the elbows waited.
The hands gripped hard on the desert.[23]

Like the other three poets, Stafford locates himself and his values in nature. But his landscapes—the endless plains of Kansas and the immense forests of the Pacific Northwest—are more vast, less domesticated than theirs, and in fact the self Stafford places in them locates itself partly by vanishing into them, letting that self be absorbed into what is rustic and enduring and ungovernable. For Stafford, it is a great comfort to "live in a hemisphere beyond what Columbus discovered," which you can't walk through "without wrapping a new/piece of time around you," as he puts it in the poem, *Is This Feeling about the West Real?* In contrast, many symptoms of civilization, from small talk to warfare, herd the self into the confines of groupthink where the imagination, which for Stafford is inextricably linked with conscience, withers and dies. In that same poem he cautions, "...your teakettle/and cozy life inside can deny everything outside—/whole mountain ranges, history, the holocaust,/sainthood, Crazy Horse... ."[24]

But despite his propensity to instruct us, Stafford, like Jane Kenyon, ultimately offers us an egoless, or transcended self, suggesting again and again that he is a humble messenger representing rather than possessing greater powers. At the end of this poem, the didactic speaker of the previous passage dissolves, simply blending into the grandeur and mystery of the larger atmosphere: "Listen—something else hovers out here, not/color, not outlines or depth when air/relieves distance by hazing far mountains,/ but some total feeling or other world/almost coming forward, like when a bell sounds/and then leaves a whole countryside waiting."[25]

Stafford was supremely conscious of personal, sacred space as the wellspring of his own poetry. He was also a compelling teacher whose gift expressed itself partly in his untiring dedication to helping others access the sacred spaces in themselves. In his prose writings as well as his poems, he acts as a benevolent secular leader trying to herd his flock to a place of ease and balance within themselves—to alertness and eagerness, to courage, to healing solitude—and to the joy of creating poems from that place. I offer *When I Met My Muse* by way of conclusion, and as a talisman to anyone willing to explore the risks and rewards of writing "personal" poems:

When I Met My Muse

I glanced at her and took my glasses
off—they were still singing. They buzzed
like a locust on the coffee table and then
ceased. Her voice belled forth, and the
sunlight bent. I felt the ceiling arch, and
knew that nails up there took a new grip
on whatever they touched. "I am your own
way of looking at things," she said. "When
you allow me to live with you, every
glance around you will be
a sort of salvation." And I took her hand.[26]

The two poems that follow provide an arena in which to attempt
some translation of what sacred space feels like to me. They are both
approximations, as sacred space is a shapeshifting thing, more aura than
outline, growing beyond me every time I manage to pin down a piece of it.
This is an invitation to keep trying:

Silence

Once at a retreat, all of us forbidden
speech for a day, I found myself
translating the breezes off the Pacific—
their many registers of hush
through palm and banana leaves—
and tracing endlessly the flight loops
of frigate birds, great wings hardly moving,
their dense bodies lifted on the heft of thermals.

All day I felt a lightness
widening in my chest, its membrane
pressed but not broken by the habit
taken out of reach, the impulse
I had lived by. And my eyes—
I felt them deepen, washed bluer,
pouring over the others a calmness

so strange to me
even as I drew each of them in
along with the sun that sifted through
our hair and thin shirts, and the dusk
that settled around each face
as we ate dinner outdoors, cushioned
in our deep privacies—I could have drifted
forever in that shared restraint

but one man found it too much.
How sadly, then, I returned
to my known self and lost the depths
my eyes had claimed, lost the greening
of my thoughts and lost, until
now, most memory of those hours
without speech.

Library of Small Happiness

Sunlight early in the day
is expectant. Experimental. Liquid
slanting across the just-waking room.
Now a page is opened, and the mind—
the heart?—turned gently as a glued
spine cracks, well-made thoughts
taken out and taken apart
and the night's fast still
unbroken—a pleasure to leave
flesh free of bread's weight
as time, too, stays weightless
and the room hums with light—a voice rises
from the page toward the voice within
or maybe it's just from within.
It shapes the hours to come—

O expectant, silky morning, O lion
lying down with the lamb
as though the room were forest
replete with moss and ripe fruit—
word-clouds lift the body
inside the body. Weightless and without
demand. So heaven must be
like this, free of purpose, and lit
with intelligence that needs
no proof. The body weightless
and without demand.
Each taken-apart thought
remaking itself and going where
it's never been, the mind (the heart?)
such a fine book, cracking
and cracking its spine that never breaks.

A SPIRAL WALK THROUGH THE GOLDEN MEAN

*F*rom the marginal doodles that curve from wrist to pen and bring a sense of kinetic pleasure as one sits on the phone or at a meeting, to the giant ground drawings of Ancient Nasca in Peru, the spiral has made its way, often mysteriously, to surfaces familiar to us. It is not a static shape even when represented two-dimensionally; it invites us to touch, to trace, to travel. Phenomena such as labyrinths and the Spiral Jetty, a contemporary and often-submerged work of landscape art located at one end of Utah's Great Salt Lake, pull us into the paths they etch, and they gain dimension as the elements etch layers of another history onto them. The dance form known as Contact Improvisation teaches both bodies to move in spirals in order to maintain their connection, and restorative practice of Tai Chi opens the muscles and refines balance through a sustained flow of spiral movements. Motion, process, and the passage of time are inherent to the nature of spiral. It is holographic and endlessly compelling.

The spiral has also surfaced, in the form of shells and fossils, from underwater, underground, and deep history. Walk into any gem store and you'll see them, especially the Nautilus ancestors known as ammonites, polished and gleaming under lights. When they are sliced, the flat inner side reveals a plate of chambered segments spiraling outward to chronicle an ancient creature's expansion of its home. Over a period of 350 million years, these chambers have filled with hardened sediment, compressed time, forming an inlay of earth tones as intricate and lovely as anything made by an artist. I have been unable to resist acquiring a large number of them. I've made some into pendants to wear, sell, and give away, an activity which has given me the oddly pleasant feeling of being a conduit rather than an owner or creator.

Recently, a friend who owns one of the pendants observed that the ammonite's appeal can be explained, in part, by the fact that its proportions replicate the ideal proportions established by the Pythagorean-Platonic theory of numbers known as the Golden Mean. This observation set me, a writer trained almost exclusively in the Liberal Arts, on a foray through the Internet to learn something of the language of mathematics. The foray now has become a spiral in its own right, giving me an increasingly expansive understanding of the workings of nature, art, and especially of *process* in all its momentum and mystery.

❦

The Golden Mean is fairly easy to understand with the help of diagrams. If you bisect a straight line in the "golden" place, the ratio of the lesser segment is to the greater as the greater is to the whole, at a ratio of 1:.618. If you turn the shorter segment up 90 degrees you get two sides of the "golden rectangle," whose proportions can be seen in playing cards envelopes, and magazines and are said to form the most visually satisfying of all rectangles.[1] This ratio, also known as Divine Proportion, has morphed into pentagrams and pyramids and onward into complex designs by Michelangelo, Leonardo da Vinci, and the builders of the Parthenon, as well as works by modern masters such as Le Corbusier and Mondrian.

Although nature does not work in straight lines, it does work with surprising frequency in patterns closely related to the Golden Mean. One of these is the Logarithmic Spiral, an orderly spiral which gets farther from its point of origin by a factor of .618 with each quarter turn it makes. Another is the series of "golden numbers" known as the Fibonacci sequence (named after its thirteenth-century discoverer) in which each successive number is the sum of the two previous ones: 1, 1, 2, 3, 5, 8, 13, 21, and so on. After the first few numbers, the incremental increase between the numbers begins to stabilize approximately at the ratio of 1:.618 between the larger number and its immediate predecessor. These Golden Mean-related patterns turn up in the movements of hurricanes, the swirl of planets in galaxies, the pattern of seeds on the head of a sunflower, the proliferation of leaves in numerous plants,[2] and the ammonite, which can measure anywhere from a half-inch to six feet across.

As my friend initially pointed out, the ratio between the line that reaches from the center to one side of the ammonite's spiral is to its overall width as that of its width to its overall length. More exciting to me, however, was my subsequent discovery that an ammonite not only snuggles right up against each side of a golden rectangle, but each new rotation of the spiral, starting at the smallest point of origin, fits inside its *own* golden rectangle. As the shell expands, then, each of its segments grows larger but keeps the same proportions as its predecessors, culminating in a predictable and visually appealing sequence that can clearly be seen from the inside, a celebration of a close relative of the Logarithmic Spiral known as the Golden Spiral.

Not long ago, another friend suggested I read Phyllis Levin's beautifully documented introduction to her anthology, *The Penguin Book of the Sonnet*, because it mentions the Golden Mean in relation to the construction of this enduring, generative poetic form. Indeed, Levin's introduction did much to expand my understanding of Divine Proportion as it relates to the lyric poem; i.e., to the trajectory of meditation as it leads to insight. But I didn't expect that so many of her images and observations about the sonnet would also call forth the structure and energy of a spiral, especially a spiral inhabited by a past or present living creature. In addition to introducing the sonnet as "a monument of praise," Levin adds in the same breath that it is "a field of play, a chamber of sudden change."[3] She explains that "stanza" means "room,"[4] which makes me think of Nautilus chambers and the pattern made by their progression as analogous to the unfolding of thought marked by stanzas and rhyme clusters. Here are a few of Levin's other spiral-resonant observations about the sonnet:

The sonnet contains and enacts "tension between a fixed formal pattern and endless flow of feeling."[5]

The sonnet is "a blueprint for building a structure that remains open to the unknown, ready to lodge an unexpected guest."[6]

The sonnet is tightly contained while paradoxically "amplifying patterns of image and thought."[7]

And finally, I was reminded that an ammonite is not just a dynamic physical object but also a venerable one whose past remains visible today, when I encountered Levin's observations about the sonnet's long history in conjunction with the variations it is able to sustain in the hands of contemporary writers:

> Since its overall dimensions and circumference do not change, whatever occurs within that space will always be determined to some degree by its size and haunted by the presence of its former occupants. Even if we rearrange, replace, or remove some of the furniture, the marks will still be there to remind us of how things were positioned in the past.[8]

Levin's essay highlights the role of the *volta*, the turn, a rhetorical change in strategy that dramatically informs the shape and trajectory of thought in the sonnet, even as it has a significant role in other forms as well. Not coincidentally, she tells us, the placement of the *volta* in many fourteen-line sonnets occurs at a Golden Mean-related divide, at or near the eighth line, making the infrastructure of the sonnet asymmetrical regardless of how it looks on the page. The first eight lines as they relate to the following six provide what she terms a "dynamic" structure by making the sonnet "top-heavy." And, she continues, "Opposition resides in its form the way load and support contend in a great building."[9]

The placement of the *volta* is most evident in the Petrarchan sonnet, which originated in Italy in the 1300's and contains two quatrains and two tercets in which each pair of stanzas incorporates identical rhyme schemes. The most obvious turn in an English sonnet occurs at the final couplet, which traditionally is rhymed and preceded by three quatrains, each of which contains its own rhyme scheme; nevertheless, Levin maintains, an identifiable rhetorical shift frequently appears near the eighth line in an English sonnet. Thus the English sonnet, which evolved from its Petrarchan predecessor primarily because English cannot sustain identical rhymes as Italian can, "still carries the traces of its ancestry—not only in the number of lines determining the form, but also in the place where the Italian sonnet registers a change that can feel seismic in so small a space."[10]

Seismic or not, moments of change in even the English sonnet may well arise from the poet's instinctive sense of proportion in the flow of argument or revelation, an instinct that often is implemented through rhetorical conventions. For example, the ninth line in Shakespeare's *Sonnet 29* begins, after a semicolon at the end of the preceding line, "Yet in these thoughts myself almost despising," thus signaling a shift from his preoccupation with his "disgrace with Fortune and men's eyes" to a celebration of "thy sweet love," the thought of which makes him conclude, despite his former gloom, "I scorn to change my state with kings." His *Sonnet 18,* which begins, "Shall I compare thee to a summer's day?" and proceeds to celebrate his love's "temperate" virtues that place her qualities above the more intense and short-lived qualities of summer weather, sets up a significant shift in its ninth line: "But thy eternal summer shall not fade." This both intensifies the contrast he has established and sets up the platform for the more dramatic turn in his final couplet: not only are his love's qualities more enduring than those of nature, but his tribute to them, embodied in this sonnet, assures their immortality.

Of course there are many variations in both the placement and the function of the *volta* in the sonnet form. I am less interested in reducing the sonnet to formula, which sonnets generally refuse to tolerate anyway, than I am with using the sonnet to illustrate how the lyric mind may be tuned, via registers it may be only subliminally aware of, to the dynamics of Divine Proportion. Here is an unrhymed, unmetered sonnet by William Stafford whose trust in the associative process, free of conventions or intent, is legend:

Time

The years to come (empty boxcars
waiting on a siding while someone forgets
and the tall grass tickles their bellies)
will sometime stay, rusted still;
and a little boy who clambers up,
saved by his bare feet, will run
along the top, jump to the last car,
and gaze down at the end into that river
near every town.
       Once when I was a boy
I took that kind of walk,
beyond the last houses, out where the grass
lived, then the tired siding where trains whistled.
The river was choked with old Chevies and Fords.
And that was the day the world ended.[11]

Stafford's fourteen lines have the flow and physical appearance of a Petrarchan sonnet, making a significant shift from the platform set up by the first 8 1/2 lines, in which both the metaphor of time as a series of boxcars and the general harmlessness of a boyhood ritual are established, to the brief flashback that leads swiftly to a particular boy's loss of innocence. However, the final two lines, offering the sudden image of a river composed of ruined cars instead of water, followed immediately by an epiphany that offers no way out, effects the tight closure of an English sonnet—and all this, from a poet who described his approach to writing in the following terms, in his seminal essay, *A Way of Writing:*

> …receptive, careless of failure, I spin out things on the page.
> And a wonderful freedom comes. If something occurs to me, it
> is all right to accept it. It has one justification: it occurs to me… .
> I know that back of my activity there will be the coherence of
> my self, and that indulgence of my impulses will bring recur-
> rent patterns and meanings again.[12]

At the time, 1970, Stafford's intuitive approach to the writing process was fresh and liberating. The methods he introduced to poets, which involved "trust" and "forgiveness" as well as the discipline of addressing the blank paper every day, have become cornerstones of the pedagogy for teaching composition as well as creative writing. But for our purposes, Stafford's sonnet offers an illustration of how nature's forms may well reside within us and make their way, unbidden or quasi-bidden, into poems. This brings us back to the function as well as the placement of the *volta*.

Levin considers the *volta* as nothing less than "the seat of [the sonnet's] soul."[13] And it plays not just a structural role but also something related to timing and motion, to choreography within the poem, which can draw reader as well as writer into the cohesive swirl of its elements:

...the reader's experience of this turn...reconfigures the experience of all the lines that both precede and follow it... . Likewise,
the poet's anticipation of the *volta* guides every move he or
she will make. The moment a pebble is dropped into a pond,
evidence of that action resonates outward, and at the same time
continues to draw the eye back to the point from which all
succeeding motions ensue.[14]

I enjoy contemplating the point of origin from which the ancient
cephalopod began to build its circular home as analogous, in its *effect* rather
than its function, to a kind of *volta*, drawing the viewer's eye simultaneously into and out of that center. This offers another way to account
for appealing tensions inherent within the ammonite's form, and for the
complex but unmistakable harmony it achieves overall—which, as Levin
demonstrates, is exactly what a sonnet does.

In other poetic forms, this effect of simultaneous inward/outward
tension has less to do with mathematical proportions or with strategically
placed turns than it does with patterns of accretion and repetition. My for-
ays into the Golden Mean, as they drew me more deeply into contemplation of the Golden Spiral, kept inviting me to explore the *sensations* aroused
in me by a spiral, taking me away from math into the realm of phenomenology. I began to recognize spiraling sensations in poetic forms that rely
heavily on repetition and only peripherally on turns—sestinas, pantoums,
and villanelles—as their repetitions build dynamic structures and rhythms
that often hold the reader in a kind of vortex, drawing her aurally towards
a center and then flinging her onward and outward, moving to expansions
of their patterns but never breaking the tegument, the music, of the poem.

My investigations into the Golden Mean led me to two other particularly interesting documents by poets, which support my instincts about the profound but less measurable implications of the Golden Spiral as it relates not just to finished work but to the process of its making. One of these documents is John Frederick Nims' chapter on "Golden Numbers" in his seminal poetry textbook, *Western Wind*. The other is Paul Lake's essay, *The Shape of Poetry*, in *Expansive Poetry & Music Online*. Both writers did much to help me progress from formulas and diagrams into the workings of nature. Nims cites the way rabbits breed, the generation of bees, the number and pattern of leaves or petals on certain plants, and the opposing spirals not only on sunflower heads but also on pinecones and pineapples. Lake mentions the growth of human organs, snowflakes, tornadoes, and bird wings.

Both poets discuss how poems in various forms can replicate golden proportions not only in their structures, but also in the way they unfold for the writer. Nims mentions patterns of "living growth" that take place over time, such as the incrementally curling horns of mountain goats, elephant tusks, cats' claws, and the beaks of parrots, and he likens these spirals-in-progress to the way poets create stanzaic structures out of an instinctive awareness of "continuous proportion."[15] Lake cites an interview with Richard Wilbur, who maintains that he never starts out with a preconceived form but rather commits himself "to the metrical precedents which [his] first lines set... ." This gives him, he says, "an advance awareness" of how long a poem is going to be, what its tone will be, and which of its rhythms and line lengths will be "capable of repetition without troubling the flow of thought as it emerges."[16] Wilbur can sense all of this before he knows just what the remainder of the poem will contain or how it will end.

Lake also cites an experiment, by computer scientist and behaviorist Craig Reynolds at the Santa Fe Institute, which has yielded provocative new information about the flocking behavior of birds and possibly about other "complex natural systems," including shifting sand dunes and living trees.[17] A computer was programmed to direct the movements of images

A Spiral Walk Through The Golden Mean

called "boids" by programming the response of each boid to the objects in its immediate vicinity, be they other boids or obstacles scattered randomly in the field. He programmed the following behaviors:

1. That each maintain a minimum distance from other objects in the environment, including other boids.
2. That each match velocities with boids in its neighborhood.
3. That each move towards a perceived center of mass of boids in its neighborhood.[18]

What Reynolds didn't program was a destination; these boids weren't directing each other, from a lead boid down, to hightail it to a particular tropical paradise before the weather got ugly. Yet a flock did indeed form, evolving simply from each boid's response to objects in its neighborhood, a phenomenon that began from the bottom up. The flock remained intact and resilient, instantly "collecting" itself even when it had to split to fly around an obstacle.

Lake cites other chemical and meteorological phenomena to highlight what he describes as "nature's surprising ability to self-organize holistically, through a complex and sensitive system of feedback, into an emergent new form."[19] Bringing time into his discussion of "non-linear dynamic systems," he touches upon fractal geometry and also upon the role of chance supplied by environmental feedback,[20] which explains something about coastline and cloud formation even as it takes us farther, without separating us, from the Golden Mean *per se*. It illustrates to science-deficient people like me how profoundly we, as creatures who are also "emergent natural forms," may find some things "beautiful" and others not. More importantly, the notion of "emergent natural forms" can help us better understand what goes on when we engage in the oft-studied but difficult-to-pin-down process of making art, a process fueled by *felt* rather than defined intention, and by focused instinct. Perhaps this explains how even in the moment—perhaps *especially* in the moment—a good jazz musician senses how long a riff should take to build to a crest and then how long it should take to diminish, and Abstract Expressionist painters like Robert Motherwell and Jackson Pollack were able to trust the wave of energy that guided their brushes or paint-spatters across a canvas to tell them, by its natural diminishment, that the painting was "finished."

※

As a writer and teacher, I have long been familiar with the stages of creative and intellectual processes. "Brainstorming" and "clustering" have become common terms for the initiation of experimentation and incubation which eventually yield the discovery and refinement of a subject, as well as an organic structure to serve its various elements. Perhaps this process can be seen as traveling backwards through a spiral, starting big and tightening inward, even as the brainstorming process begins movement outward from and around a center. Much has been written by educators and psychologists about this progression, but that vibrant stage of ignorance and trust, the dynamics of uncertainty interacting with a sensed but undefined goal, are more difficult to articulate. The best I have been able to say of my own experience of this process is that something always happens if I "show up and wait." It's something I repeatedly have to remind myself to do despite the articulate reassurances offered me early on by William Stafford's *A Way of Writing*.

Recently, while I was clearing a bookshelf, a little pamphlet titled *The Creative Process: A Study in Paradox* literally fell into my hands. I don't remember who gave it to me or when. It was written by Charlotte Lackner Doyle, a psychology professor at Sarah Lawrence, and the essay it contains originally was delivered as a lecture in 1975. Doyle, who specializes in the psychology of creativity, gracefully summarizes the theories passed down from Freud, Jung, and Maslow, who offer different terms and explanations for this phenomenon in which "primitive processes" as well as craft and skill come into play. She also offers terms that have become more familiar in our culture in the thirty-five years since she wrote the essay, "flow" and "divergent thinking."

While honoring these precedents, she ultimately goes beyond them to describe the paradoxes of the creative process more precisely yet holistically than I have ever seen. She is aided in this endeavor less by the stalwarts in her field than by some of her then-colleagues: fiction writers Grace Paley and Katherine Anne Porter, poet Jane Cooper, and composer Joel Spiegelman, all of whom she interviewed for her essay and cites throughout.

Combining her ample background in psychology with an artist's openness to the insights offered by her interviewees, she arrives at the term *total centration,* which she defines as "the most marvelous, mysterious and, so far, nameless part of the creative episode." The preparation for this condition "begins with the intimation that the process has begun, with a hunch that there is a seed of thought…a germ that starts the process…the intuition that there is something to work on… ."[21] In the next and often lengthy stage, she explains, the artist "thinks through his medium," which is not the same as logical thinking, or a translation of something extraneous to the medium into the medium, but rather a direct transcription of the mind-in-motion, aided by craft, into images or characters or paint or musical phrases. "The medium," she says, "is a kind of reality principle. It shows us when we don't know what we think."[22] And it becomes the vehicle by which we figure out what we think.

This sets the stage for total centration, a phenomenon which normally doesn't happen all at once but occurs in starts and stops, bracketing periods of uncertainty, exploration, and even discouragement, while a work is being realized. Nevertheless, Doyle maintains, it is a distinct stage of endeavor, characterized by alchemy rather than effort, when elements and insights seem to fall or fly into place:

It is the period…when the characters take over, when the melodies flow without forcing, when the painting seems to paint itself… . All the awkwardness that comes from watching yourself at work, from the fear that what you are doing is no good, from careful critical selection, is no longer a part of the flow of thought and action… . This total centration is a particular kind of consciousness. I am not speaking of a drug state; in fact, I suspect that a sustained period of total centration might be almost impossible under drugs… .

During periods of total centration, self-in-the-world, as a way of organizing experience, no longer pops in recurrently. For extended periods, the organization, the flow and change, is determined by the object or the task on which attention is centered…*its* direction and *its* structure… .

During the period of total centration, all the patterns of the mind are potentially active. There is a center towards which all the activity flows, and I believe that center is neither the personal nor the collective unconscious but that growing object in the world, those developing ideas-in-flesh, developing in relation to that initial intuition which started the creative episode and the goal of articulate statement in the medium. This is the magnet that attracts and patterns all those resources which become available.[23]

Every time I read these passages, I experience a physical sensation of spinning in a contained space, and of pressure both inward and outward. It is a marvelous sensation, and it remains barely explainable even with the help of Doyle and others who have done so much to articulate it. When I encountered her rendition, sitting cross-legged in front of a half-emptied bookshelf, I recognized its truth immediately, as would anyone else who makes art in any form. But the real revelation, for me, was and remains its implicit description of how a spiral looks and acts.

A Spiral Walk
Through The
Golden Mean

101

The Golden Spiral has become a friendly sort of ghost that accompanies me everywhere lately, having grown beyond the diagrams and printouts and theories I've been poring over. It finds its way into my twilight sleep. It superimposes itself over my eyes as a flash of recognition when I look, say, at a reproduction of Georgia O'Keeffe's *Jimson Weed,* even though I don't know if "divine proportion" applies mathematically to its sunburst spread of creamy petals. I feel the dance of it in the waves of associative thought that come naturally when I jog along the rim of the Valdez Valley, where the cottonwoods themselves seem to be spiraling deeper and deeper into their season of gold.

Even with the help of Doyle's essay, I don't really understand, nor am I able to trace, just how my own poems evolve from a few sketchy phrases into holographic meditations. But I now have an image for a dynamic I have always sensed: how the kind of associative thought that begins with and then adheres to a felt sense of focus does indeed replicate the effortless, organic unfolding of a spiral. A swirl of motion that occurs continually within us and outside us. A blueprint that gives rise to, even as it is enlarged by, our instinct for beauty. To contemplate all this is to feel some of the old promise return, that state of beginner's mind that allowed many of us to discover, before we got serious, how fine it felt to arrange and rearrange words, to handle them and be handled by them, to fashion our first poems and stories pleasure by pleasure.

This poem arose quite some time after I wrote the Spiral Walk essay. I was using some lines of my own as a prompt, which became the title, and the snail simply appeared, inviting more of the world in:

Folded in on Itself

Two antennae finger the sunlit air
hesitating, nearly blind, through moisture
and shades of light, towards the promise
of something green. Such risk
to the soft body made mostly of water
but for the durable house it carries
everywhere—it can wind itself back, any time,
and there resides in a perfect architecture,
labyrinth of chambers curving inward, its legacy
left in millennia of sand, water, and stone.
Ammonite. Nautilus. Common snail.
Maker of proportioned chambers measured
and uplifting. Parthenon. Cathedrals
plotting the progress of faith through Europe—
did mankind know exactly why this pleased
the eye? Sunflower, ram's horn and fiddlehead fern,
God's eye replaying the world in its image. Spiral.

"ALL THE SOFTNESS TRUTH REQUIRES:"

SPECULATION AS INVITATION AND PERSUASION

*S*peculation in any genre, but especially poetry, can position the speaker to approach the inexplicable, the ineffable, sometimes the unspeakable, without sounding reductive or overbearing. Gestures like "Perhaps," "Maybe," "Suppose," "Is it possible that...?" allow a writer to "make" major points via suggestion, and to enjoy the powers of an imagination unfettered by the obligation to ground itself in prior authority. The imagination loves this. It swells to fill the greater space. Often, the reader does too; the rhetoric of speculation allows a writer to walk around a subject or idea, to mull over small, incremental observations and to invite the reader directly into the search and its ultimate revelations.

When I think of the deft, subtle powers of speculation, I'm reminded of Peter Falk in *Columbo,* a TV show popular in the '60's, which featured a slouchy, sloppily trench-coated detective who tended to mumble and look perplexed and ask a lot of questions. His manner utterly disarmed the people he questioned, especially the cool, collected guilty ones who saw no threat in him whatsoever. At the end of a seemingly inept interrogation that disguised his inductive reasoning, an interrogation accompanied by much head-scratching and furrowing-of-the-brow, he would start to leave and then turn around with a final "Oh—and one more thing"—then *bam*, his final question, disguised as the inevitable conclusion, would nail the truth. "Where *did* you buy the poison that killed your wife?"

We poets are not detectives. We are not always trying to prove something, but more often are trying to tease something out. Thus, while Columbo's methods offer an endearing example of a "soft" approach to truth, an even softer approach can be made when a poet hasn't yet identified what she's after. "I didn't know any word for it," writes Elizabeth Bishop in *In the Waiting Room*, a poem first published in her collection, *Geography III*, that meticulously renders a young girl's first experience of the arbitrariness and fragility of her existence as "an Elizabeth." For a few moments, small details of the world around her take on such sharp clarity that she becomes unrecognizable to herself. In this poem, "I didn't know" becomes fertile ground for all that surrounds it, a series of speculations and outright questions which do more to encompass the enormity and existential weight of her experience than any analytical effort or a series of statements might do.

In the Waiting Room depicts the speaker outside a dentist's office reading **National Geographic** while her aunt is being treated behind closed doors. Two elements converge to cause the speaker to leave her body and fuse with a vastness she can scarcely grasp: her aunt's soft exclamation of pain overheard from inside, and the images that rise from the pages the speaker is reading: "a dead man slung on a pole," "babies with pointed heads/wound round and round with string," and "black, naked women" whose breasts strike her as "horrifying." These images bring her face to face with a primitive, human reality utterly foreign to her and, along with her aunt's soft cry, they catapult her into a strange, limitless space, a kind of vertigo: "…you are an I,/you are an *Elizabeth*,/you are one of *them*./*Why* should you be one, too?"

The heart of the poem, then—the passage in which the speaker descends most deeply into her altered state before resurfacing to the familiar world—is rendered entirely through questions:

> Why should I be my aunt,
> or me, or anyone?
> What similarities—
> boots, hands, the family voice
> I felt in my throat, or even
> the *National Geographic*
> and those awful hanging breasts—
> held us altogether
> or made us all just one?
> How—I didn't know any
> word for it—how "unlikely…"
> How had I come to be here,
> like them, and overhear
> a cry of pain that could have
> got loud and worse but hadn't?[1]

These questions evoke an experience for which the speaker has no words, though she uses words to re-play its immediate and progressive impact. The questions have no answers, which makes them all the more compelling to a reader who consents to the invitation to participate directly in a few life-changing moments happening to someone who herself doesn't understand them.

Often, a question can work more directly as revelation, a culmination, an arrival at insight that has grown from prior observations and speculations. This can be seen especially when a poem ends with a question; for example, in Robert Hayden's *Those Winter Sundays*. The first stanza describes the speaker's father getting up early mornings "in the blueblack

"All The Softness Truth Requires:" Speculation As Invitation And Persuasion

107

cold," before everyone else, to build a fire "with cracked hands that ached/ from labor in the weekday weather." In the third and final stanza, we learn he also polishes the speaker's Sunday shoes. But the middle stanza refers to "the chronic angers" of a house in which the family speaks "indifferently" to one another or not at all, implicating the father in an emotional chill that contrasts with his dawn ritual of bringing warmth to the rooms before his family wakes up. Hayden does not need to explain or resolve this contrast, but his final gesture releases strong feeling and thus works as epiphany, honoring as it does the silences and services the poem has depicted: "What did I know, what did I know/of love's austere and lonely offices?"[2]

Betsy Sholl uses speculation both as insight and as a method of circling something too big for containment, the Holocaust, in her poem *After That*, which appears in her collection, **Late Psalm**. Its epiphany-like ending consists of a series of questions that dismantle any possibility of a God who has control over the actions of mankind. In addition, she manages to evoke what can't really be described about the persistent shadow of the Holocaust, without ever mentioning the word itself or the standard horrors associated with it. Instead, she works the contrast between a young speaker and a group of old widows who somehow have ended up in Lakewood, New Jersey, and in the process, she offers a careful selection of deft, glancing images that add up to more than the sum of their parts.

The speaker is an adolescent girl preoccupied with makeup and shoes dyed to match a prom gown, passing a hotel porch full of old Jewish women who rock in their chairs, "sputtering like those old newsreels of Europe,/where they must have walked through snow/in battered boots with newspaper socks,/looking for streets that no longer existed." The girl, to whom the present is all that's real and for whom the future still holds promise, feels at once judged and dismissed by "the chorus of mourners lined up,/davening in wicker chairs/…cradles endlessly rocking the world's woes,/dividing by who saw from who shut their blue eyes." Indicted by her youth and her own "blue eyes," she feels her life shrink in the shadow of what she grasps as the women's burden of memory. The final stanza, then, driven by questions along with images that etch more deeply the history of these survivors, manages not only to further dismantle the speaker's life (no surprise there), but also to reduce God himself to her level of helplessness:

> ...I can't
> enter a store without hearing their voices—
> so much vinegar even God would shudder,
> would rummage through bins, wanting
> to give them something, anything at all,
> those fierce widows rocking forever
> on the guest house porch, refusing to enter,
> refusing to leave, having outlasted whole cities.
> What would you ask after that—
> Some bright pleasure, a new truth?
> Loden green pumps with stiletto heels?
> That the world end, that the world continue?[3]

Sholl's poem not only manages to contain the unspeakable, but it ends by *uttering* indirectly, through her final series of questions, what people who adhere to traditional religions might well consider blasphemy. But without the barb, without the defiance. God is simply caught up in the mess, and the poem gathers Him in its wave of compassion.

Both Hayden and Sholl write themselves *into* their most powerful questions. Sometimes, however, a question or speculative gesture can provide entry to a poem that spins *out* of them, as in Stanley Kunitz's poem The Abduction, from his 1971 collection, **Passing Through**. It begins: "Some things I do not profess/to understand, perhaps/not wanting to... ." He then goes on to recount a childhood incident his wife has described to him, most likely a rape ("you stumbled out of the wood/...your white blouse torn/and a bloodstain on your skirt") but which together, fueled by her will to "believe," they have reconstructed into something magical and transformative: "how you encountered on the path/a pack of sleek, gray hounds,/...and how you were led, through leafy ways,/into the presence of a royal stag,/...who kneeled on a swale of moss/before you; and how you were borne/aloft in triumph through the green... ." In this case, the inventions wrought by the speaker and his wife touch upon another aspect of speculation as it defines a genre formally called Speculative literature, which is not the subject of this essay but applies somewhat to the work of speculation in Kunitz's poem. Speculative fiction and poetry in their own right work off of fantasy and invention, veering into the realms of science fiction or fairy tale, though neither of these terms does justice to a genre that is versatile and still evolving. Speculative literature can be humorous, satiric and, at its best, over-the-top but eerily convincing. In Kunitz's poem, the speaker and his wife invoke similar fantasy-making energy as they fashion an alternative version that transcends simple denial of a traumatic event; however, their version weaves its own spell, fashions its own myth. Near the end, the speaker observes, "...even now,/when I hold you in my arms,/I wonder where you are./...you lie beside me in elegant repose,/a hint of transport hovering on your lips... ." Whether or not he believes their shared invention, he nevertheless understands it has acted on his wife as real experience, and thus on him as well, calling into question so much more than what actually happened in that vanished "childhood country." He ends the poem with a question that adds depth to, rather than answering, his opening question: "What do we know/beyond the rapture and the dread?"[4]

When inserted inside the body of a poem, rather than at the beginning or end, questions can drive and deepen the poem's structure, giving it the energy of a Socratic give-and-take, even—or perhaps especially—when the answers slant away from the questions or don't match them at all. Many of Robert Creeley's deeply interior poems, for example, with their abbreviated moments of perception, defy logic but manage to coalesce around a central question (usually an unpunctuated one) followed by a gesture that serves as an answer simply because it *feels* like one. The speaker of his iconic poem, *I Know a Man*, driving and speaking manically to his friend about "the darkness" of their condition, asks, "what //can we do against/ it..." and "why not, buy a goddamn big car... ." This question occurs in the third stanza of this four-stanza poem consisting of twelve very short lines. Directly following, the fourth and final stanza reads: "drive, he sd, for/christ's sake, look/out wher yr going.[5] His friend's directive, an ostensibly practical one that applies to the situation at hand, nevertheless serves as a response to the speaker's existential meanderings. It could be taken as something like "stay in the moment—what other choice do you have?"

Others of Creeley's poems such as *The Business, The Language,* and *The Window* are a little longer and less oblique, allowing the reader to work through initial bafflement at a lack of obvious connection between question and resolution to begin to grasp instead how the question in the middle or latter half of the poem serves as a *volta*. It draws the reader into the search and allows both poem and reader to re-structure Creeley's flow of perception into an arrival that feels, once one has deliberated a bit, somewhat cohesive.

In other cases—for example the expansive Whitmanesque flights of supposition and visualization in many of Pattiann Rogers' poems— questions and speculations can provide a rhetorical structure of logical argument while the details themselves are wildly sensuous and illogical. In such poems, improbable elements are juxtaposed and fused in a manner reminiscent of a Magritte painting, or a Jerry Uelsmann photograph fashioned from multiple negatives. In her long poem, *The Importance of the Whale In a Field of Iris* from her collection **The Firekeeper***,* Rogers drives each new riff, each new burst of incantation and visualization, with phrases like "If someone may assume...," "And doesn't the iris, by its memory of whale...," and "If they hadn't been found naturally together, who would have thought to say… .?"[6] Of course the whale and the field of iris have no relation to one another, but by the time the reader has followed the poem through its unspoolings of imagery, its sinuous sentences, and its utter abandon to the act of imagination, all of which are connected by gentle, leading gestures of indirect logic similar to Columbo's, the reader is likely to find herself won over.

Another of Rogers' poems from *The Firekeeper*, *When At Night*, uses the repetition of phrases initiated by "suppose" to spin out an erotic fantasy of being ministered to by tender woodland spirits. It begins, "Suppose all of you came in the dark,/each one, up to my bed while I was sleeping.// Suppose one of you took my hand/without waking me and touched my fingers… ." Subsequent stanzas begin with "Suppose two of you were at my head, the breath/of one in my ear like a bird/moth thuddering…," and "Suppose another drew the covers down to my feet… ." This last "suppose"-driven clause is followed by a beautifully choreographed progression of imagined ministrations, all quite gentle, that result in imagined orgasm, although that word is hardly an appropriate label for an act in which these spirits "guard" and "protect" the speaker, and react sympathetically to "equal [her] trembling." The final stanza drives the speculative tone of the poem to further heights and then lands it quietly with a final question. It also offers an example of the rich, self-propelled energy of Rogers' visualization and long, sumptuous sentences:

And at dawn, if everything were put
into place again, closing, sealing, my legs
together, straight, the quilt folded
and tucked to my chin; if all of you
stepped back, away, into your places,
into the translucence of glass
at the window, into the ground breezes
swelling the limber grasses, into the river
of insect rubbings below the field and the light
expanding the empty places of the elm, back
into the rising black of the hawk deepening
the shallow sky, and we all woke then
so much happier than before, well,
there wouldn't be anything
wrong in that, would there?[7]

The poem ends chastely, pulling back from its seductions as though they never happened, but leaving everyone—well—"happier."

Denise Levertov's poem, *The Wings*, from her 1963 collection *The Sorrow Dance,* is driven entirely by questions, offering a layered series of speculative gestures that create a tone of genuine doubt even as they grope their way towards a threshold of greater certainty and, ultimately, a tentative ownership of power. The speaker is addressing a "you" to whom she defers, and who seems to have been threatened by the very qualities she is seeking to tease apart and redeem in herself. The use of speculation in this poem is more raw and fundamental than it is in Columbo's cagy set-ups, and less elegantly crafted than it has been in the poems mentioned so far. Rather, Levertov submerges us directly into a soup of uncertainty, and even after she has groped her way out of it somewhat, she still seems genuinely cautious. Her use of line and stanza breaks reinforces the hesitations of her thought process, offering a stellar example the "organic" use of form she illuminated and made popular in the numerous essays she published in the 1960's and '70's:

The Wings

Something hangs in back of me,
I can't see it, can't move it.

I know it's black,
a hump on my back.

It's heavy. You
can't see it.

What's in it? Don't tell me
you don't know. It's

what you told me about—
black

inimical power, cold
whirling out of it and

around me and
sweeping you flat.

But what if,
like a camel, it's

pure energy I store,
and carry humped and heavy?

Not black, not
that terror, stupidity

of cold rage; or black
only for being pent there?

What if released in air
it became a white

source of light, a fountain
of light? Could all that weight

be the power of flight?
Look inward: see me

with embryo wings, one
feathered in soot, the other

blazing ciliations of ember, pale
flare-pinions. Well—

could I go
on one wing,

the white one?[8]

Having had the good fortune to meet Levertov later in her life, and having benefitted richly from her essays on line breaks and organic form as well as from her poems, I must say my experience of her was that of a woman in full command of herself, a woman far more comfortable with her powers than the speaker of this poem seems to be. But I am touched by the struggle and the urgency, chronicled so beautifully here, of a woman working her way through hesitations and doubts to a cautious claim to her own turf, a private sort of Feminism. She still defers to that anchoring "you," but the reader can see she is ready to fly.

The title of this essay, *All the Softness Truth Requires*, is borrowed from William Stafford's poem *Lit Instructor* (quoted on page 80), from his collection, **The Way It Is**; the phrase comes from his description of himself standing before his students "beating my wings/with all the softness truth

115

requires." The students themselves, more attuned to the efficacy of "force" and "battering," "shrug" in response and relegate his voice to the realm of "tentative things." Stafford, however, whose generous and certainly speculative essays and poems enriched scores of writers and students during his long career as a mentor, understands his efforts as a "dance" towards "knowing." He especially values "stray error" as its gift, a reclamation of something "lost" which he can coax "home" with his own figurative wing-flutterings. For Stafford, exploration is the essential act. It yields knowledge in such a way that the *quest* for "truth" and *truth* itself become inextricable from one another, fusing the softness of quest with the sharp edge of certainty. "Every quick feather asserts a just claim./It bites like a saw into white pine,[9] he writes near the end of his poem, distilling the paradox I have explored incrementally throughout this essay. In just this manner Columbo feathered his way towards unassailable truths. We poets can do this too. Or we can elect to take flight, riding the question or supposition or a "perhaps" like a magic carpet that allows us to swoop and circle, to answer the invitation to explore unexpected landscapes and then return to make surprising yet unassailable landings. It is very possible that our best moments in writing, our best endings, and our most irresistible beckonings to the reader arise from curiosity. Conviction may follow. Or not.

Against Diffuse Awareness

Do not speculate on the destination of
the plastic bag blowing across the parking lot
or how the queen-sized mattress ended up on the freeway.

Do not let your mind stray, midway
between freezer and microwave, to
contemplate how every gadget in your
kitchen, every digital number
and bleep, has been extracted from rock
or water. Vanished fire. Wind.

Do not dwell on random motion, wave-particle
duality, thermodynamics, or any other
commotion going on in the air you breathe,
the water that runs over your hands,
transformations ubiquitous and fleeting as the glint
of a shod hoof disappearing in the sun

Do not stare into vacant lots in the middle of cities
like Chicago, with their bald spots and empty cartons
and weeds gone out of control, each detail
a whole genealogy of neglect—or try to
imagine the vast roots that once reigned there
as branches held their poise, like the arms
of flamenco dancers, in hard rain.

Do not pause at the sound of someone
weeping quietly—say, behind a newspaper
on the train, in a phone booth or a restroom stall—
as each exhalation, having gathered itself
from a rare moment of communion
with the soul (which for that moment is not
an abstraction) suspends itself.

*"All The Softness
Truth Requires:"
Speculation As
Invitation And
Persuasion*

Forget this story—just one of many that crowd
the dumping grounds of what you insist
you don't have time for—about a peasant
who helped build the great cathedral at Chartres,
who sluiced dirt from his tired body one evening
and stood before his hut, letting his mind
roam with the crickets and sheep. As the stars
faded, his thoughts lifted him
from himself and set him down
as rough quarried stone, as gold
in the priest's coffers, as prayer on the lips
of a new widow, as the play of light beyond
a tunnel etched behind the eyes of his newborn son
who in his own lifetime would not see the cathedral finished.

PRESS SEND:

RISK, INTUITION, AND THE TRANSPARENT POEM

I had never thought of "transparency" as a quality with enough substance to offer fodder for a discussion about poetry until I heard Ron Padgett read his poems and then use the word in an informal talk. At the time, I was in the midst of an experience still new to me: that of writing a poem a day to paste into an e-mail every night to a group of other writers. I had begun this with misgivings—expecting to worry the poems or run out of subjects. Instead, and increasingly, I felt like an athlete discovering and strengthening muscles, stretching instincts for association, and molding my material into arcs in one sitting. Every night I felt a release of exhilaration as I pressed "send." Padgett's description of his swift and unpremeditated writing process, coming as it did in relation to my tentative new enterprise, made something more click into place for me.

I had been experiencing my own poems-written-under-pressure as calisthenics rather than accomplished moves, but the exercise itself felt increasingly meaningful. Faced with the necessity to complete some sort of journey on the page last thing before bed, I found myself moving more swiftly, wielding lighter tools, and savoring the pleasures of travel. With increasing frequency, I found myself in territory that surprised me and, even better, I experienced a liberating lack of self-consciousness. None of those in my group was expected to comment on anyone's work, and in fact we were under no obligation to even read it. Of course we did read it, but the removal of expectations—all the expectations I had internalized for over thirty years of writing and teaching writers—turned out to have a profound effect on me.

Hearing Padgett read his work, I marveled at the subtle authority of his poems despite their apparent offhandedness; I found them exploratory, wise, amused by self and world, and subtly layered. They offered registers of tone and pacing I recognized as faintly echoed in my own uncharacteristically swift attempts. And it occurred to me that revision of my new work could be in service to an attempt to preserve the appearance of ease and spontaneous discovery rather than to disguise it with adornment or expansion. After his reading, Padgett made an offhand remark about exchanging poems once with Donald Hall, sharing his mild disbelief that a "brocaded" poet like Hall should have any interest in a "transparent" poet like himself. By "transparent," Padgett was referring to use of language that does not depend on form, sound-work, metaphor, condensation, or complexity of thought—apparently straightforward language like that used by William Carlos Williams. But the notion of "transparency" began to resonate for me beyond a description of language into possibilities for describing process as well. It gave me a point of departure for further exploring the sensations I had stumbled upon while sending nightly poems to friends.

Padgett's poems carry themselves with ease and lightness, but they also find arrivals along the way, moments that invite a reader to reflect and reread. In this sense, they bear weight that seems to be no weight at all. The ending of the following poem instantly wins my trust and invites me to go back and recognize how every seemingly offhand remark along the way has led up to it:

Walking with Walt

When everyday objects and tasks
seem to crowd into the history you live in
you can't breathe so easily you can hardly breathe at all
the space is so used up,
when yesterday there was nothing but.
Ah, expansive America! you
must have existed. Otherwise
no Whitman.

It's funny that America did not explode
when Whitman published *Leaves of Grass*,
explode with amazement and pride, but
America was busy being other
than what he thought it was and I grew up
thinking along his lines and of course now
oh well

though actually at this very moment
the trees are acting exactly the way they did
when he walked through and among them,
one of the roughs, as he put it,
though how rough I don't know I think
he was just carried away

as we all are, if we're lucky
enough to have just walking
buoy us up a little off the earth
to be more on it.[1]

The poem unfolds playfully, making and then undercutting its own speculations, creating friction between each gesture in a crisp debate with itself until it seems to talk itself into a dead end at "oh well." Then it's off and running again, fueled by yet another contradiction, an assertive turn that catapults the flow of thought towards greater sureness as it makes increasingly swift connections between the speaker's and Whitman's times until they are one and the same. At this point, the trajectory of thought seems almost to have moved ahead of the speaker, the poem itself having taken over. The speaker's voice remains casual and speculative throughout, but the pacing picks up as the elements introduced in the first half of the poem—the references to Whitman, spaciousness as opposed to busy-ness, and America past and present—narrow swiftly to closure that holds them and more, just as the earth continues to hold and "buoy" us in spite of our preoccupations.

The apparent spontaneity of Padgett's reflections conveys speed, the sensation that the poem is a seizing-of-the-moment rather than a product of prior deliberation. Transparent poems such as this one, then, favor momentum over a layering of elements. Consider Frank O'Hara's frenetically transparent poems, which replicate the manic pace and sensory overload of living in New York City, and the advice he gives, in his famous anti-manifesto, *Personism: A Manifesto*, to "just go on your nerve."[2]

O'Hara's "manifesto" is manifestly irreverent, yet it also states what is essentially true for him: "…you have to take your chances and try to avoid being logical. Pain always produces logic, which is very bad for you."[3] The transparency in O'Hara's work is radical, headlong, and flippant to the brink of self-dismissal, yet it never quite loses sight of an implicit purpose, often *gravitas*, which reveals itself in bits and shards along the way. Repeatedly, he arrives at observations that stop and provoke the reader; then he takes flight again. "I'm not saying that I don't have practically the most lofty ideas of anyone writing today," he writes, " but what difference does that make?…The only good thing about it is that when I get lofty enough I've stopped thinking and that's when refreshment arrives."[4]

Refreshment is one of the objectives of the transparent poem—refreshment first for the writer. Reading O'Hara, I often have the impression that unless he's amusing himself in the moment, he could be overcome by some kind of undertow; that for all the social and improvisational energy he seems so delighted by, he is also trying to outrun or resist something that threatens that energy. This is where "nerve" comes in. The very title of one of his most surreal pieces, the prose poem *Meditations in an Emergency,* reflects the adrenalin-fed nature of some transparent poems. The transparent poem is indeed an act of meditation, but sometimes meditation under pressure, forming itself via its own momentum rather than rhetorical scaffolding, and rising to meet whatever rears before it, "emergency" or otherwise.

My own favorites of his poems, like the one below—and like my favorites of another of his cohorts in the New York School, John Ashbery—reveal snippets of a distinct, if paradox-laden, aesthetic behind their apparent offhandedness, and these snippets serve to guide the reader into some intuitive grasp of these poems' intent:

Poetry

The only way to be quiet
is to be quick, so I scare
you clumsily, or surprise
you with a stab. A praying
mantis knows time more
intimately than I and is
more casual. Crickets use
time for accompaniment to
innocent fidgeting. A zebra
races counterclockwise.
All this I desire. To
deepen you by my quickness
and delight as if you
were logical and proven,
but still be quiet as if
I were used to you; as if
you would never leave me
and were the inexorable
product of my own time.[5]

O'Hara reinforces my own sense of the "quick" linked with the "quiet" of composing and reading a transparent poem. In addition, this poem works somewhat in dialogue with, and perhaps as an enactment of, O'Hara's oblique hints at an *ars poetica* in *Personism: A Manifesto*. I have difficulty explaining these connections, but I can *feel* them in the evident sleight-of-hand relationship between poem and reader that reveals a poem as elusive, perhaps flirtatious, yet an undeniably *present* phenomenon. A thing that almost self-destructs but maintains its shimmer. In poems like the one above, O'Hara treats the reader as a co-collaborator, someone on the other side of the flirtation and who might well return some of the provocations the poem serves up. "Personism," O'Hara says, "puts the poem squarely between the poet and the person, Lucky Pierre style, and the poem is correspondingly gratified. The poem is at last between two persons instead of two pages."[6]

II

In its quieter manifestations, as in Padgett's work, the transparent poem can be disarming, conversational, and to a degree easy to grasp in one sitting, but rich with implications and reverberations that expand during subsequent readings. It is often speculative. The transparent poem takes what it is at hand, which more often than not is the accessible stuff of quotidian life, and makes it fresh. Pushes it a little beyond its expected territory. The transparent poem appears to be written by someone, or at least a persona, unencumbered by prior assumptions, unconscious baggage, or the sort of ennui that can paralyze—someone motivated by curiosity and often daring. The transparent poem is supple and sure, like a cat scaling a tree or stalking something that moves invisibly through deep grass. It seems always to know where to place its feet.

William Stafford, who encouraged a generation of writers and teachers in the 1970's to compose poems in a spirit of "trust and forgiveness," left a large body of poems and essays that prove such trust is warranted. His New and Selected volume, *The Way It Is*, issued by Graywolf in 1998, remains classic and warming: substantial proof of what can bloom when a poet disengages from the nearly continuous cacophony of doubts, fears, and the voices of others, and simply falls in with the pleasures and rhythms and provocative open-endedness of the work itself. Stafford speaks as a kind of elder, someone with values to impart, but his poems consistently also offer fresh imagery, language, and leaps of thought that allow a reader to dream alongside them and participate in the surprise encounters the poem allows itself. His poem, *A Little Gift* (quoted in its entirety on page 82), recounting an imagined reciprocal absorption as he watches and is watched by big circus cats being unloaded from a train, ends with the lines: "I let any next thing fold/quietly into the blackness that leads/all the way inward from the hole in my eye."[7] They offer a succinct rendition of his process of receiving and then building on images that present themselves to him.

The receptivity Stafford advocates, and demonstrates in his work, has continued to exert influence through his dozens of poetry collections and his two volumes of published essays. Having recommended him to my students during my long teaching career, I have yet to encounter one who didn't feel grounded and renewed after spending time with his brief, much-anthologized essay, *A Way of Writing* (from which I have quoted on page 95). It transcends movements and fads, politics and po-biz, and it nudges the writer towards resources that are innately his or her own. It is the clearest prose statement I have found about how it feels to write a transparent poem.

Certainly, there are risks inherent in transparency as I am using the term. The most obvious is that a finished transparent poem can easily be a thin poem, a poem that is too easily satisfied with itself and will not sustain subsequent readings. A fine line exists between a poem that *appears* simple and one that proves upon subsequent readings that indeed it *is*. Often, one can't know on which side of the line one's new poem has fallen. In addition, writers like Padgett, Stafford, and O'Hara, all of whom have written swiftly and prolifically, don't always hit the mark. Or they hit it with varying degrees of success. But at their best, all three in their different ways make swift, surprising journeys towards closures that reverberate beyond themselves, and many of their poems spring off the page with remarkable ease. Anne Waldman, in a blurb that appears on the back cover of Padgett's 800-page *Collected Poems*, calls him "a genius." Although Padgett himself surely laughs off such a label (as would Stafford), perhaps it does take a certain genius, or at least inspired confidence, to ride so repeatedly those precarious waves of meditation and associative flow and, more often than not, make a solid landing. Stafford would say it simply takes practice, advocating the virtues of allowing oneself to "launch many expendable efforts."[8]

Another risk is that transparency, in relation to process, can easily be said to be not-so-new, turf already turned not only by Stafford in his essays in *Writing the Australian Crawl*, but also by Robert Bly's revival of Surrealism in *Leaping Poetry*, by the Abstract Expressionists who revolutionized American art in the late 1940's through the 1960's, and by the New York School of poets who admired and wrote about them.

And finally, many writers achieve qualities of transparency as I've described it through a great deal of deliberation and revision, evoking the impression of swiftness, grace, and spontaneity that only appear to have turned up on the page with scarcely a ripple of effort. There are many factors involved in such sculpting, paring, and deep listening—factors worthy of another essay entirely—but I suspect that some of the energies of transparency, often accompanied by an attraction to classic Eastern forms such as haiku and haibun, have informed the apparent effortlessness and the crispness of association these writers achieve via careful selectivity.

So is the "transparent" poem a new phenomenon? Is it a distinct phenomenon? Yes and no. It invites a re-exploration of Stafford's advice to writers in the late 1960's, and also, especially, it invites another look at the Abstract Expressionist movement among New York artists more than a decade before. There's something to be said for revisiting, through a perspective gained by distance, aesthetic movements that broke considerable ground in their day before they settled into the categories assigned them by critics and scholars. In addition, the notion of transparency and the qualities it implies offer a refreshed lens through which to view some kinds of paintings and poems and as well as essential aspects about the process of making any kind of painting or poem. For us, as poets, it is not necessarily a better lens but one that places particular emphasis on the audience as full partner in a dance, a trajectory of incremental discoveries. After the more cerebral and identity-based aesthetic movements that took place in the 1980's and onward (and these movements were necessary, inevitable pendulum swings), it brings us back to the organic.

III

The seeds for the many mid-century movements in poetry were sown, or at least prefigured, by painters and sculptors who found themselves in New York right after World War II and loosely formed an approach to painting that later came to be known as Abstract Expressionism. These painters were, among many things, very physical in the presence of their canvases, and watching them on film adds a new dimension to works that lack immediately recognizable subject matter. Jackson Pollock literally danced around the huge canvases he spread on the floor, alternately deliberating over them and flinging paint. Robert Motherwell's spare, slower brush strokes involved his whole body—the arc of his arm, the bending and straightening of his waist—and even if one can't "get" such paintings, even if one can see no decipherable images in them, one can see on film the intimacy between the living body and the marks appearing on the canvas, marks which now take on meaning as motion. Once cognizant of the physical movements chronicled by the art, the viewer can stand before the canvas and feel their presence on the canvas itself. It's no surprise that the Abstract Expressionists called their movement "Action Painting."

Action Painting, then, was "transparent" painting, inviting the viewer immediately into the gestures and turns of energy leading to a sense of arrival or completion. And likewise, transparent poems such the ones O'Hara was writing during that time—a time when he also was writing about these painters for *Art News*—can also be experienced as "action" poems. The interchangeability between the processes of making paintings and making poems is reflected in O'Hara's famous poem, *Why I Am Not a Painter*, which actually manages to counteract the implications of its own title by choreographing a *pas de deux* and eventual union between his friend's work and his own:

Why I Am Not a Painter

I am not a painter, I am a poet.
Why? I think I would rather be
a painter, but I am not. Well,

for instance, Mike Goldberg
is starting a painting. I drop in.
"Sit down and have a drink" he
says. I drink; we drink. I look
up. "You have SARDINES in it."
"Yes, it needed something there."

"Oh." I go and the days go by
and I drop in again. The painting
is going on, and I go, and the days
go by. I drop in. The painting is
finished. "Where's SARDINES?"
All that's left is just
letters, "It was too much," Mike says.

But me? One day I am thinking of
a color: orange. I write a line
about orange. Pretty soon it is a
whole page of words, not lines.
Then another page. There should be
so much more, not of orange, of
words, of how terrible orange is
and life. Days go by. It is even in
prose, I am a real poet. My poem
is finished and I haven't mentioned
orange yet. It's twelve poems, I call
it ORANGES. And one day in a gallery
I see Mike's painting, called SARDINES.[9]

This poem is an example of what O'Hara called his "I do this, I do that" poems. But he creates something of a metrical pattern through his comings and goings chronicled via short staccato sentences and use of repetition. And the poem makes a satisfying full-circle, one whose trajectory holds up for a reader moving more slowly through the poem than O'Hara himself appears to move. As a rendition of a process that serves to illustrate a seemingly disheveled aesthetic, the poem nevertheless demonstrates considerable craft, reflecting as it does the energies and disciplines favored by artists whose work only appeared to have no rules or rigors behind them.

"I paint a lot by correction,"[10] said Robert Motherwell, a prominent figure among the Abstract Expressionists and the subject of a fine documentary, *Storming the Citadel*. He made his initial brush strokes or set down collage pieces swiftly enough, but then questioned and edited, asking himself all the while, "Is this the truth?" For him and the other painters in his circle, "truth" existed at some distance from the starting point of a piece—unanticipated, growing from the materials at hand and from the gestures of the artist, stumbled upon and finally *recognized*. For Motherwell, "The game is not what things look like. The game is the organization of states of feeling."[11] One of the best educated and most celebrated figures of the Abstract Expressionist movement as well as its articulate spokesman, Motherwell simply said of his work, "I don't know how to paint a picture but I know how to paint the *experience* of painting a picture." [12]

Motherwell taught at Black Mountain College in the early 1950's, where he crossed paths with Black Mountain poets Robert Creeley, Charles Olson, and Robert Duncan, all of whom had some access to the restlessness and excitement occurring on the New York scene and were engaged in parallel paths of their own. Creeley chronicles this fertile time in his essay, *On the Road: Notes on Artists and Poets, 1950-65*, which he wrote as a reflection on the evolution of his own aesthetic and that of his compatriots.

Like the painters, these poets had come of age just after the Second World War when, as Creeley recalls, "...one felt the kinds of coherence that might have been fact of another time and place were no longer possible... the arts especially were shaken and *the picture of the world* that might previously have served them had to be reformed."[13] Creeley understood that the choice before him was either paralysis or experimental movement in an attempt to "gain location in the insistent flux, recognizing the nature of its shifting energies as intimate with one's own." He continues:

> ...this situation increasingly demanded that the arts, *all* of them—since no matter how disparate their preoccupations may sometimes appear, their roots are always fact [sic] of a commonly shared intuition or impulse—...that the human event itself be permitted to enter, again, the most significant of its own realizations.[14]

This "human event," like that defined by the Abstract Expressionists, involved a revolutionary and necessarily personal, feeling-based experience of process that, as Creeley puts it, "made both the thing said and the way of saying it an integral event,"[15] something he first came to appreciate through his conversations with Charles Olson. Once he found a community of like-minded souls at Black Mountain, Creeley settled on his true course, guided in part by the visual artists he met there:

> ...I hadn't as yet realized that a number of American painters had made the shift I was myself so anxious to accomplish, that they had, in fact, already begun to move away from the insistently *pictorial,* whether figurative or nonfigurative, to a manifest [sic] directly of the *energy* inherent in the materials, literally, and their physical manipulation in the act of painting itself.[16]

Creeley's essay goes on to offer quotations from his Black Mountain compatriots, and also to reference figures such as O'Hara, Robert Rauschenberg, and John Cage in ways that illuminate the shared intentions of artists across the spectrum, along with their excitement in re-evaluating the purpose of art. It is a wonderful document for anyone interested in the qualities of transparency as I have described them, but for now, I would like to offer an example of Creeley's own brand of transparency, his own "manipulation" of his "materials" in the interests of re-creating the experience of perception in its moment. In the following poem, he questions the nature of perception itself, suggesting the possibility that it could be the perceiver who arranges objects in the outside world, and not the other way around:

The Window

Position is where you
put it, where it is,
did you, for example, that

large tank there, silvered,
with the white church along
side, lift

all that, to what
purpose? How
heavy the slow

world is with
everything put
in place. Some

man walks by, a
car beside him on
the dropped

road, a leaf of
yellow color is
going to

fall. It
all drops into
place. My

face is heavy
with the sight. I can
feel my eye breaking.[17]

Creeley's short lines give the impression that he can't help but interrupt himself as one perception begins to crowd into another. In the process, coherent thought breaks down, as does coherent syntax, leaving a re-creation of perception groping its way, fragment by fragment, towards something approaching a revelation—perhaps the kind of revelation that directly precedes a more finished thought. Like so many of Creeley's works, *The Window* is driven by speculation and even contains a direct question, and its thoughts never really finish themselves until the very end, where they culminate in an observation or assertion that serves obliquely as an "answer." This provides structure to a poem that may appear, at first glance, to have little or none.

Denise Levertov, who sustained lively dialogues and friendships with Duncan and Creeley, did much to spread the influence of the Black Mountain poets in her essays as well as her poems, legitimizing terms such as "open forms" and "organic form" that were embraced throughout the 1960's and 1970's as creative writing classes became increasingly popular in college English departments. She differentiated "free verse," which most writers and teachers at the time viewed as an absence of rules, from "organic poetry," in which decisions about form are inextricably intertwined with content:

In organic poetry the metric movement, the measure, is
the direct expression of the movement of perception. And
the sounds, acting together with the measure, are a kind of
extended onomatopoeia—i.e., they imitate not the sounds
of an experience (which may well be soundless, or to which
sounds contribute only incidentally)—but the feeling of an
experience, its emotional tone, its texture. [18]

Levertov wrote eloquently on metrics, sound patterns, and line breaks, opening up myriad ways in which they could be used to render "the feeling of an experience." And she did much to help writers understand the power of white space in a poem, the power of pauses as well as text in underscoring what she called the "exploratory" nature of most organic poems. Her poem, *Stepping Westward*, like Creeley's *The Window*, replicates a groping towards arrival, though Levertov's poem is more coherent as she works her way not perception by perception, but more question by question, arriving at partial answers. Ultimately she arrives not at *the* answer, but at an increased sense of resolve:

Stepping Westward

What is green in me
darkens, muscadine.

If woman is inconstant,
good, I am faithful to

ebb and flow, I fall
in season and now

is a time of ripening.
If her part

is to be time,
a north star,

good, I hold steady
in the black sky

and vanish by day,
yet burn there

in blue or above
quilts of cloud.

There is no savor
more sweet, more salt

than to be glad to be
what, woman,

and who, myself,
I am, a shadow

that grows longer as the sun
moves, drawn out

on a thread of wonder.
If I bear burdens

they begin to be remembered
as gifts, goods, a basket

of bread that hurts
my shoulders but closes me

in fragrance. I can
eat as I go.[19]

*Press Send: Risk,
Intuition, And The
Transparent Poem*

137

Levertov's line and stanza breaks in this poem isolate her fragments of thought, enjambing where the thought is uncertain, feeling its way, end-stopping briefly with commas wherever thought finds at least temporary purchase, and ending with periods only when thought reaches some sense of conclusion. It is an exquisitely textured poem, varied in its rhythms and sustaining its energy line by line, couplet by couplet, by isolating small, incremental moments of distinct recognition and revelation within each border of white space. Like the work of Creeley and O'Hara, it is transparent in its intimacy and apparent spontaneity as it effects a seamless fusion between something happening in the writer and something happening in the reader.

As should be clear by now, none of these poets or artists was alone in inventing this particular wheel—perception and experience used as the implicit subjects of art—though perhaps the Abstract Expressionists were innovators to the greatest degree, starting as early as they did and exploring their territory passionately, in isolation and often amid derision, eschewing the most enduring traces of Renaissance influence, well before their work took hold on the public. Nevertheless, something clearly was in the air during that long postwar period, and artists in all genres drew inspiration from many sources, past and present, that tilted them in similar directions. Motherwell references Kierkegaard, Mallarmé, and Alfred North Whitehead, among others. Levertov draws from architects Louis Sullivan and Frank Lloyd Wright, as well as Emerson, Thomas Huxley, Whitehead, and of course her contemporaries who taught at Black Mountain. This list could go on, plucking some threads from the ancient Greeks and Romans. The point is that the "something in the air" reverberated widely throughout the arts, pulling disparate elements into a more or less common sensibility the way a tuning fork settles musicians into key.

Other developments in American poetry of the 1950's and 1960's placed value in many different ways on the direct transfer of personal experience, organic uses of form, and spontaneity, as can be seen in most of the major movements of the time. The Confessional poets used personal experience as a primary medium, breaking the then-prevailing Modernist aesthetic of detachment. The Deep Image poets, influenced by Surrealism, used the subconscious as a medium. The Black Mountain poets used the body, including breath and the physical choreography of thought and perception, as a medium. The New York poets used experience, perceived and immediate to the point of appearing undigested, as a medium. The unifying factor was that writers in different camps emphasized some aspect of personal feeling and/or perception as a means of locating the self not only in a world that recently had undergone devastation and was under the unprecedented threat of nuclear destruction, but also in a culture that now was in a process of unprecedented growth, prosperity, and change. All of these developments laid the groundwork for what I've been calling "the transparent poem."

IV

One of the things that struck me while writing under pressure every night was the sensation of reaching intuitively after some kind of trajectory leading to closure: tension evoked and then resolved, or tension leading to revelation if not resolution, or some other kind of change resulting in a diminishment of energy that felt like completion. I suspect that anyone who loves to read, not to mention someone who teaches literature or writes, has internalized a sense of form through repeated exposure to plot structure and the arc of lyric meditation without even knowing she has done so—that an innate sense of pattern, breaking-of-pattern, sometimes-return-to-pattern, and closure are indeed hard-wired in us.

And there is something even more internal, as Stafford suggests in *A Way of Writing*—something connected to who we *are* over and above *what we've learned*. "...I know that back of my activity there will be the coherence of my self," he says, "and that indulgence of my impulses will bring recurrent patterns and meanings again…. ."[20] Perhaps, then, from both within and without, we have access to instincts that have everything to do with transparency in its application to process as action and action as subject. No accident, then, that a transparent poem might swiftly be made to work, or can at least reveal movement and structure that are clear enough to guide the writer easily into subsequent revisions. We writers are backed by a phalanx of resources ready to help us when we get out of the way.

The poetry scene has taken several new directions in the past forty years, departing from a more or less central focus on process and the organic relationship between form and content to embrace movements such as Identity Poetics, Language Poetry, New Formalism, and Spoken Word. Nevertheless, the legacy of the process-oriented cluster of "schools" that flourished mid-century echoes through the work of many writers today as well as in the continued relevance and popularity of previous generations of writers and writers in translation. When I asked Padgett for names of poets he considered "transparent," he mentioned Charles Reznikoff, early Gary Snyder, Jacques Prévert, William Carlos Williams, contemporary Chinese poet Yu Jian, and W.S. Merwin. Poet Lynn Levin has suggested George Bilgere, whose most recent book, *Imperial*, offers one engaging example after another. Martha Collins' recent elegant collection, *Day Unto Day*, consists of six poetic sequences, each one consisting of poems written every day for a month.

Stafford prefigured the recently popular poem-a-day trend by writing poems nearly every day of his long life, including his last. I like to think that even as the world as he'd known it faded from his attention, he remained in the embrace of what he described in his essay as "the precious little area of confusion when I do not know what I am going to say and then I find out what I am going to say."[21] Stafford's reverence and continued wonder at the journeys writing offered him are the subjects of many of his poems. I especially recommend the following as articulate renditions of what it's like not just to write, but to live by writing, the transparent poem: *An Introduction to Some Poems, Report from a Far Place, A Course in Creative Writing, On Being Called Simple by a Critic* (see page 81), *The Way I Write, How These Words Happened,* and *When I Met My Muse* (see page 85), which ends: "'I am your own/way of looking at things,' she said. 'When/you allow me to live with you, every/glance at the world around you will be/a sort of salvation.' And I took her hand."[22]

It is easy for us, as writers, to forget the freedoms by which Stafford lived and wrote so well—to let our sense of what may or may not be in fashion, what our audience may or may not like, the pressure to be ironic and so on, drive a wedge between ourselves and what I have called elsewhere the "sacred space" we inhabit in the privacy of our explorations. And it's easy to forget that a writer's willingness to enter that sacred space, and then render what she finds there, can do much to help readers access and gain some trust in their own.

The transparent poem does require skill—the sort of skill that accrues over years of reading and revising until good instincts begin to lodge themselves in the pores as well as the brain. Certainly, the transparent poem requires craft. But it is also forgiving, allowing the writer to embrace it as a practice if nothing else. "Expendable efforts" have a vital role in the continual evolution that governs a writer's life. The transparent poem ultimately affirms and feeds the writer, regardless of its ultimate "success," generating something like endorphins. Or maybe what it generates *are* endorphins. Recently, reading these lines from *Variation on a Theme* by W.S. Merwin, I felt my own choices affirmed by the force of his gratitude for the experience his life's work has given him: "Thank you.../for words/that come out of silence and take me by surprise/and have carried me through the clear day/without once turning to look at me... ."

It would be remiss of me to withhold the rest of the poem, as it evokes so beautifully the connections between the actions of writing, the actions of living in the body, and the actions of living in the world. Loving and aging. Remembering gifts and mistakes. Celebrating powers that live within and without and seamlessly align us with something beyond our work even as it is our work that brings us to that threshold where the view opens into amplitude. It is difficult to capture this in a short lyric poem. But Merwin has done so, and he will have the last word here:

Variation on a Theme

Thank you my lifelong afternoon
late in this season of no age
thank you for my windows above the rivers
thank you for the true love you brought me to
when it was time at last and for words
that came out of silence and take me by surprise
and have carried me through the clear day
without once turning to look at me
thank you for friends and long echoes of them
and for those mistakes that were only mine
for the homesickness that guides the young plovers
from somewhere they loved before
they woke into it to another place
they loved before they ever saw it
thank you whole body and hand and eye
thank you for sights and moments known
only to me who will not see them again
except in my mind's eye where they have not changed
thank you for showing me the morning stars
and for the dogs who are guiding me.[23]

II.
Exercises

THE POETIC INVERSION

*T*he exercises that work best and most consistently for me are the ones that jolt me into using language I didn't expect to use, which then talks back to me and consequently leads me into directions I didn't expect to take. This enterprise starts with language itself, the raw material, rather than an idea or even image. These emerge later, of course, but in the beginning, the trick is to get words and phrases down on paper without having to cast about for a subject or even be in the mood for writing.

In this exercise, you write roughly the opposite of someone else's poem. Try approaching it phrase by phrase in the first draft, and don't get too hung up on doing anything "correctly." Often, there is no real opposite to a phrase, but try for a synonym for rough approximation, and don't think too hard! Do it a few lines at a time, and take breaks. At some point you'll start hearing something interesting happening in your own language and see motifs and situations begin to surface. At that point let your own poem go where it wants, and leave the original behind. In most cases, the original will have no presence in your finished product, though occasionally you may want to acknowledge a source poem:

Model Poem

After Actium: Loss Filling the Emptiness

The flowers do not move in the windless pause.
The armies are standing still before the fight.
Antony waits in the heat, so motionless
that no part of the metal he is wearing hits
another part. A man facing death. In the quiet
inside him, desire rises the way a glass is filled.
As nothingness is filled as soon as it is emptied.
As you in me now, all the time, day after day.
                                        —Linda Gregg

My first quick exercise without changes (though the piece
departed a little from conscious inversion):

Dead tumbleweeds jump to life in the start-up of wind.
The peacemakers scurry everywhere after the last battle.
Geronimo does not linger in the chill dusk, is full of motion so
the fringe of his clothing ripples as a single wave.
An animal who has escaped death once again.
In the turmoil around him, a sense of closure settles like a sky
emptying itself of snow.
A presence that disappears as soon as it has taken shape under daylight.
Like my waking dreams which try to tell me what I'm searching for,
what I'm finding, before I wake fully into my assumptions.

An early draft that began to tell me where I was going:

Dead tumbleweeds spring to life in the sudden wind.
Peacemakers on both sides scatter after the final battle.
Geronimo does not linger in the furious dusk, keeps
shifting his shape and weaving himself along the ground,
the fringe on his shirt moving in a single wave.
Once again he has evaded capture. Amidst the wounded
and the plunders and the flung commands, he feels
his eventual defeat move closer, like the gunmetal sky
emptying itself of snow which will become a memory of snow
as soon as daylight returns. Like my waking dream this morning
which tried to tell me where I once lived, what wild lands
want to claim me, before I woke fully to the usual room,
the chores, the familiar veil sewn over my eye.

An early draft ready for critiquing:

Weather

A sudden wind sweeps the encampments.
Peacemakers drop their flags and flatten themselves
against the rocks. Tumbleweeds storm the fields.
The warrior chief does not linger in this furious
dusk, just shifts shape again
and weaves himself along the ground, the fringe
on his shirt moving in a single wave.
Once again he has evaded capture.
The cries of the wounded and plunderers
grow faint now, the flung commands
already the stuff of legends
another race will pass to its children.
He can feel a confinement hovering
in his future, the color draining from
his skin, as the gunmetal sky lowers

The Poetic Inversion

and drops the season's final snow
which will become a memory of snow
once daylight grows strong enough to give it a name—
like my waking dream this morning
which tried to remind me of the endings I may have shared
with the seasons—how air and water keep
dying into one another—
before I woke fully into my room, chores, words
obscuring his footprints, the veil sewn over my eyes.

A more finished one of mine started as an inversion of Jack Gilbert's *The History of Men* but ended up being more of a response rather than an inversion. His poem, which I quoted earlier but offer again, gave me a template from which to work:

The History of Men

It thrashes in the oaks and soughs in the elms,
catches on innocence and soon dismantles that.
Sends children bewildered into life. Childhood
ends and is not buried. The young men ride out
and fall off, the horses wandering away. They get
on boats, are carried downstream, discover maidens.
They marry them without meaning to, meaning no harm,
the language beyond them. So everything ends.
Divorce gets them nowhere. They drift away from
the ruined women without noticing. See birds
high up and follow. "Out of earshot," they think,
puzzled by *earshot*. History driving them forward,
making a noise like a wind in maples, of women
in their dresses. It stings their hearts finally.
It wakes them up, baffled in the middle of their lives
on a small bare island, the sea blue and empty,
the days stretching all the way to the horizon.

The History of Women
       After Jack Gilbert

The history of women sighs
from the iron across the empty sleeves,
the exacting collars,
and edges along the porch rail.
It rises in the arc of a jump rope
then dissolves in a flurry of rhyme,
step on a crack, break your mother's back... .
It sends some children home
to the table waiting to
be set for eight, away from the fragrant
dusk, away from the last secret
whispered behind cupped hands.
Still, there are days when a girl
roams alone in her body, humming and
dreaming, a heroine among weeds and wildflowers.
When childhood ends, it is cut at the root
though for a time, the young beauties
spring lightly from buses to offices
without windows, thinking they
will always be pretty
and soon will leave town.
                       Understandable, then
that marriage appears to them
as an offer. They mean to
accept. Then they mean to make
the best of it, swimming
in a current that keeps them
in one place, smoothing Oil of Olay
over their useful hands, comforting
their mothers whose sadness
ceases to baffle them.
They wave the last child into
the evening, the first in a string
of crucible nights, and try
not to pace at the window.

Divorce leaves them stunned, supple
as leather, stranded for a time
on a long path towards love.
                              At times they see beauty
in each other mirrored nowhere in the eyes
of men, or in movies they watch when they
can't sleep. Waiting in a long line
to vote, they sense the shape of themselves
briefly, like ice cubes dropped in a lake,
though the speeches have blurred
to a long hush, waves against sand;
so history drives them inward
with the sound of someone clearing his throat.
Then one day it wakes them up
in the middle of their lives,
in a house that smells of cinnamon
or wood smoke, surrounded by a small wild yard.
Scrubbed apples drying on a cloth. The sun
just setting, gold over the valley's greens.
Silence everywhere, softening the horizon
and bringing it even closer.

FROM NYMPH TO ELDER:

BEYOND THE VIABILITY OF SEDUCTION

*S*everal years ago, I was asked to write about my process of composing a persona poem, *Calypso, Twilight,* to accompany the poem in an issue of *Poetry International.* I offer the piece now in the context of writing prompts, catalysts to be used or adapted by others. Examples of persona poems abound, in the voices of biblical, mythical, historical, and fairytale figures. Many of these have been written by women poets in an attempt not only to give voice to silent or passive characters in our literary heritage, and not only to reveal complexities behind characters initially presented as stereotypes, but also as a means for poets to write their way into visualizing new dimensions to two-dimensional figures. Sometimes this enterprise has had an overtly political (i.e., Feminist), and/or cynical agenda, for which Anne Sexton set a bracing precedent in her fairytale persona poems in *Transformations*, published in 1971. Nowadays, I find the enterprise promising for more subtle reasons, more in keeping with exploration leading to unanticipated discoveries. And as times change, the nature of those discoveries is bound to change as well, not only in the re-visioning of female figures, but of male figures as well. So I believe this remains fertile territory for poets of both genders, not to mention fun, and a refreshing relief from one's accessible self.

Calypso, Twilight

The blind stallion, having learned
my braille of leg and hand,
carries me without flinching
at the wind. His back has softened,
an extinct volcano, and my hips
hold me there, settled
by something I no longer
try to name. I am past the years

for bearing. My skin
turns to the work of wind
and salt, as the sun shortens
its arc above my diminished gardens.
I have little use for the silver-
wreathed mirror brought by a lover
who kept finding his way back.

If a wanderer should drift
ashore now and then, spent
and nameless, he will still find
in my eyes a trace of green.
Or blue. Depths in which to rest.
He will still find in my flesh
a firm *yes*, not padding
or pillow, but sinew like his—
from gathering wood for the long nights,
from sending men back to sea
at first light (they swim strongest then),

from rising alone most mornings
to light that never lies
and the continuous waves.

But this poet who tries to slip
into my skin—she bathes me
in stage light, too bright
yet too soft, scribbling in
her journal. She would have me say,
This is the dance my mothers
and grandmothers might have learned
had they slipped away from
children and set themselves loose
beneath the moon.

I give her back her words, a wish
blown like a kiss as the bloom
leaves her face, and love
leaves a jagged wake behind her.
It would do her little good

to know that lately I slip
like the breeze between the island's
tall rocks. I travel without
kohl lining my eyes,
without rare flowers
from my garden, and disappear
into rooms filled with smoke, jazz,
the braid and flow of tongues.
I walk through the teeming streets
without desire or dread, the way
the old stallion accepts
the bit and lets himself be guided
among the last of the wild iris.
the shrinking berries—
and sometimes my weakened eyes

From Nymph
To Elder: Beyond
The Viability Of
Seduction

feel immense, turning me
inside out, as a young man or woman
appears beside me
speaking slowly at first, as though
cracking the door to a vault
and is surprised at the words,
the rush of words,
the voice full of great birds lifting.

Calypso, Twilight took shape during the time I was reading Robert Fagles' then-recent translation of *The Odyssey*, whose leading women possessed supple waists and golden braids and seemed to linger indefinitely in the prime of life. Their power to deter the course of warriors or appease the gods seemed inextricable from their enduring beauty and sexual appeal. Even Penelope, an apparent widow for two decades, was pursued by suitors who expected her to produce heirs.

Re-reading the epic years later as an adult, I recalled with amusement how unquestionable all this had seemed to the high school version of me who read the Fitzgerald translation the first time around, the conventionally awkward girl whose sense of approaching adulthood was shaped by female characters offered in the pages of whatever she could get her hands on, be it required literature for English or books picked at random from library shelves. None of the heroines who accompanied me through childhood and adolescence—who served at subconscious as well as conscious levels as models in my secret life as heroine of my own quests—had gone through menopause. Now, my generation was well into middle age. And although scores of books written during our adult lives have offered picaresque, sensual, powerful, and interestingly complex older women, I began to realize that for many of us, our deepest personal myths—those roots formed by our earliest and most formative reading experiences—offered few models who might beckon and maybe even tempt us towards that region beyond beauty, beyond the viability of seduction, beyond nature's traditionally-perceived use for us.

I wanted to track one of Homer's nymphs into a stage of life where he might well have had no interest in her, and probably had few models of his own to follow. To my credit, I didn't have an agenda. I was curious to know how Calypso would present herself once I entered her uncharted territory. But on the way in, I pulled out an old poem which I had ruined by having an agenda, a poem featuring an earthy and independent middle-aged woman who was trying too earnestly to celebrate her earthiness and independence. I think I originally wanted that poem to celebrate a type of woman who had fashioned a rich emotional and spiritual life without marriage and children. But I had created a voice without character, without interesting shadows, without dimension. She still had that youthful desire to sing herself into visibility. For my new purposes, she struck me as self-indulgent in her efforts to show herself as seasoned, still-sexy, and positioned rather too securely at the helm of her own myth.

I borrowed some lines from that poem, only to feel them standing with pathetic bravado between me and this figure I was trying to envision in certain a stage of life I actually had been afraid to think about. One day, stuck once again, I decided to use my journal as a means to let Calypso tell me, if she'd consent to it, what I was doing wrong. After a bit of warm-up and paraphrase on my part ("she is past myth, she is at peace with the woman she wakes to each day and no longer needs to be particularly visible to others or even to herself"), she presented herself directly, and with refreshing tartness: "You're the one who needs me to affirm myself, to be conscious, when that's the very thing *I* no longer need to be." Her reprimand sprang me loose, especially when I put it *in* the new poem. It helped me define more honestly the relationship between me, a woman just beginning to confront sustainable losses, and this figure who had long since accepted them and moved on. It allowed me accommodate rather than put aside my projections, born from my lingering hold on

From Nymph To Elder: Beyond The Viability Of Seduction

my own youth, so that I was freer to understand the quiet freedom she had achieved—a freedom born of apparent renunciations. Now, speaking from the sidelines where at last I permitted her to be, she permitted me a glimpse of her inner life.

※

I have enjoyed exploring other iconic female figures as well, always with a sense of discovery despite the fact that so many fine poems have been and continue to be written about them. Here are my experiments with Penelope and Eve:

By Night, Penelope

unstitches the shoreline, the sea, the barely
visible mountain—all that binds her
to her halted story and to the suitors
who dwell below her chamber,
banging their goblets and cursing.
She unstitches the lambs being driven
single-file towards the banquet table.
She unstitches her flesh so that it rises, freed
from its single allegiance, the marriage bed
that would hand her like a birthright
to one of the next ones circling,
waiting to be chosen. She unstitches
their tunics while they sleep and piles them
like sand over the wine-drugged bodies.

She pulls jeweled threads from the sunrise
and later from amethyst twilight
and adds them to a garment all her own,
a cloak of breath, silk, all the hues
of weather, a cloak that bears her aloft

on what will later be understood as the beam
of meditation—each night she is swift
and ambrosial, her tears sweetening the torn
fields, the blood-dark seas, Cyclops' cratered eye.
Sometimes, from the depths of his own stupor
far away, Odysseus hears a curious singing or keening
that would press him towards a boundary
he cannot yet imagine, between his headlong quest
and the apparent stillness of the earth's flanks and inland waters.

Why She Reached

Eve wanted it more than fig
or grape or pear. More
than sweet water.
More than Adam's pavilion
of branches that floated her to sleep

above the ground each night.
More than peace, she wanted
gleam and shadow, the chafing
that would make her dance with
the dark—she wanted the earth

to pull hard at her feet.
The serpent was her own
mind waking, refusing
not to match that bell
that ricocheted through the trees—

the apple throbbing
with juice and trapped
sunlight. Its taut skin
split against her
teeth, the "yes,"
the first hard act,

*From Nymph
To Elder: Beyond
The Viability Of
Seduction*

and she savored it while Adam
slept, and God took in
her flex. The light that followed her
like smoke. Then He said, *Now*

you will hold this great
darkness; your body will swell
with all you know. You will
bend to its rotations,
its expulsions,

its nights of no sleep
and your mate will dance
around you in a fury,
his feet seeking hold
in whatever he can borrow.

So she bears it, every
seed and drop of juice,
fills her plate,
bleeds it out, cries out
in labor but not

when his hand strikes her face.
When she sits awhile with
other women, they exchange
glances like a handshake.
They lean into each other,
their voices low bells
and soon they laugh, they
laugh, they lace the air with
trickery and joy, the juice
aged to bite back, hard cider.

FIRST LINES BY OTHERS:

A LEAP INTO FRUITFUL SPACES

Several years ago, shortly after the MFA Program at University of Texas-El Paso officially became a bilingual one, I was introduced to a substantial bilingual anthology, *Twentieth-Century Latin American Poetry* edited by Stephen Tapscott, which I selected as a text and began to read dutifully in preparation for my first bilingual poetry workshop. I soon became less dutiful, more enchanted and then irresponsible, as the energy in those poems entered me like a tonic and made me itch to write poems of my own rather than think about my class. I was particularly seduced by elements easiest to preserve in translation—swiftness of association, a delicious mixing of the senses, astonishing juxtapositions, and incantatory rhythms. Occasionally over the next few weeks, I plucked someone's first line from the collection and simply let fly, trying for a swift free-write launched by borrowed energy. Then I went back to my usual dogged mode, reworking the material at length to better serve the surprises and revelations I'd stumbled upon.

Over the years I have done this exercise sporadically, taking breaks so as not to wear it out, though I have come to trust that much of the time it is likely to work both for me and others. I especially am drawn to the way it thrusts me into a technical situation I have to write my way out of, like Houdini escaping yet another enclosure. If that first line is a question, do I let it grow into a list of questions, or do I try at the outset to answer it? If the first line is a sentence fragment, how am I going to transform it into a beginning passage with sufficient momentum? Do I let it run to a whole litany of sentence fragments, and if I do, what happens when it runs out of steam? If that first line is a reference to something said by a character, very possibly then my job is to let that character keep speaking—to invent a rich enough inner landscape from which he or she might have more to say entirely apart from what he or she said in the original poem. Sometimes a first line gives me a point against which to argue, regardless of the fact that at first I don't know what or why I am arguing.

I've found this exercise works especially well in a group setting, in addition to serving as a good catalyst for my own work. After lugging the Tapscott anthology to a remote fishing village in Mexico one year, I discovered that a legal-sized sheet containing first lines without their accompanying poems worked just as well, although by then, the book had become a good friend, and I missed having it around.

This exercise, like others that work best for me and often for other writers, supplies an occasion to arrive at language that takes us by surprise and urges us, at least at first, to listen more to it than to the selves we brought to the task. As we sustain a dialogue between ourselves and the surprises in our tones and language, we do enter ourselves, of course—but through the back door, through hidden rooms, through new configurations of memory and imagination. It is not difficult to keep those first lines and correctly honor their sources. I italicize the borrowed first line and acknowledge the source in an epigraph, as can be seen in the examples that follow.

Birth Day

After a line by Homero Aridjis

To emerge from woman is to
become separate
from the ease of
floating. From water
as air—that first sunset
could be sky ripping itself apart,

calling back the ruin of flesh.
To emerge from woman is to
look back just once at a calm too deep
for words, before turning to
the startled faces, white stones
huddled around the shore of it

and the voices that rise
among them, noise without shape
and a darkness called *night*
that might feel safe if it were
water, not air, edgy
and full of eyes. Years

will pass before amber lights winking
in the hills are a comfort.
Before a grid of bone and muscle
can be trusted to hold
the body in its own axis—
to emerge from woman is to be

ambushed by the wonder
and burden of limbs. The first time
a hand, a leg is dragged
upward, the world begins
again and suddenly
is spinning, has always

First Lines By
Others: A Leap
Into Fruitful Spaces

167

been spinning, such effort
it will take to stay aboard! Years
will pass before one's wails, wrenched
from a sadness whose depths
close overhead and will never
be crested, arrange themselves

into word and phrase
and a barely supportable silence.
To emerge from woman
is to feel the throat drowning in air
and for a long time to be
afraid of water.

The Mutable Heavens

> After a line by Carlos Drummond de Andrade

When I was born, one of the crooked
angels who live in shadow, said: I, too,
knew what it meant to meet the wind
with straight bones, with skin
that held light. I breathed its song
set free over string and polished key;
I drank my share of kisses
that happened first
in the mind, and left an aftertaste
of expectation; for years
my limbs gave new shapes
to air, thrilling in sockets
that lost a little moisture every year... .
The others press forward now, their
faces smooth trinkets flickering against
the night whose velvet is deeper, more
treacherous than you know. You'll forget
mine was one of the first faces you saw—

a flash of beaten, darkened gold—
until one day you'll awaken to an ache
where the fingers bend, a thickening
that traps the ring with its carnelian sun;
your leg suddenly heavy on the stair;
leaves falling quietly in all seasons
from healthy trees (will you learn to love
the holes they leave, the rent fabric
through which night pours in?);
the surprising range of an old diva's voice
rising beyond the crevice that quietly has split
your life down the middle; your house
breathing again, every autumn,
once the weeds are cut down.

*First Lines By
Others: A Leap
Into Fruitful Spaces*

JUXTAPOSITION AND THE GIFTS OF BRILLIANT
SURPRISE: THE BRAIDED POEM

*T*he desire to write with freshness, energy, and insight is a daunt-
ing aspect of the drafting process, especially when we think we have to do
all the heavy lifting ourselves. But once juxtaposition becomes part of the
process, the resulting friction between elements yields startling moments
whose rightness can be recognized by us writers, and consequently by our
readers. These moments seem to be gifts, but they've come from surprising regions in ourselves, and we can stay in those regions as we experiment
further through revision. This is, in part, the legacy of Surrealism, but not
the sort that sought to derange the senses. Rather, juxtaposition can show
us what compelling things can happen when we *re-arrange* the senses.
Examples can be found in photographs by Jerry Uelsmann and paintings
by René Magritte as well as in poems by Swedish poet Tomas Tranströmer
and by many Latin American and Spanish poets. Robert Bly's book,
Leaping Poetry, has relevance here as well, although his agenda is somewhat different from my own.

This exercise involves simply alternating lines taken from two different poems which, when it works, results in an energetic braiding of motifs.

1. How to generate material to be braided:

Start with a first line by another poet and let it take you somewhere. Do this for one or both segments. Use one or two spare drafts of your own. Use one or two poems by other people; this is, after all, at least at the outset, an exercise.

Draft a new poem that invites you to use the senses in new ways; i.e, describe an emotion or feeling or other abstract quality in terms of a particular color or material or physical sensation (back pain/snow, for example, or empathy/thorn pricks, or resolve/the color blue). Or set up a sense-based exercise with a question like "What does a feather sound like?"

There are limitless other possibilities. It's important that you allow these exercises to *be* exercises, and to not worry about honing them too much unless one of them seems to want to be a poem of its own. You're after energy here, not perfection.

2. Braiding

Try to allow yourself to get into a zone where you don't worry too much about whether you're giving equal play to both poems. Don't try for a system. You may feel inclined break up phrases and alternate them, or to alternate between whole sentences, and/or even to keep some longer passages intact. You may change tactics as you proceed. The "zone" aspect of this is that you may well find yourself floating above both poems and hearing the third poem very early on; let that new voice inform your decisions, and let yourself work quickly. You can always go back and do the whole thing again.

Another approach is to write both the preliminary exercises in fairly short or medium-length lines, and then try alternating the lines themselves when you draft the third piece. You'll have to do a lot of editing to smooth out the syntax, but you'll get some exciting material as well.

You can keep others' first lines, if they work for you. Just italicize them in the body of the poem and add an epigraph under the title, "After a line by…" as described in the previous exercise.

3. Your own fused piece:

Once you've got your initial "exercise" version, there are limitless possibilities. So allow yourself to depart significantly from your sources, or to take one part and run with it, or re-do your combinations if the energy seems not to be working. You may also decide to keep whole passages from one of the sources more intact than the exercise originally allowed. There is no wrong way to do this—and this includes you finally deciding to jettison one piece and keep the other.

4. The point?

You may or may not get a usable poem from this, though you're likely to if you stick with it. But for sure, you will allow yourself the satisfying experience of generating new material and becoming un-self-consciously absorbed, focusing on language for its own sake, and feeling your own resources grow a little richer as you tap them. I've discovered that "showing up" is the most important thing we can do as working writers. We don't have to be in the mood, we don't have to be feeling all that good about ourselves at the moment, we may not have a thing to write about; but somehow, showing up and staying a while can break through the dullness and allow something unexpected to happen. It is so easy to forget this. Unless you're feeling really recalcitrant and/or depressed (in which case you should probably read some fun trash or go to a movie), this exercise is one way in which you can surprise yourself into a substantial work session.

Juxtaposition
And The Gifts
Of Brilliant Surprise:
The Braided Poem

Two

After lines by Carlos Pellicer and Gabriela Mistral

The taste of October on your shoulders
distracts me from your reasonable gestures
of seduction. *I have in my throat one*
word, but I don't know the sound of it,
only that it feels like breath along
my cheek. Or a hand over mine.
You might think your kiss and a few
endearments have softened me;
it's the word I don't know
to which I seem to surrender.
I find myself on a strange
path that involves my hands
and yes, your skin, which becomes
landscape for the search. A word
surrounded by phantom sound. Dunes
beneath my palms. A string of syllables
with no beginning. Something large in the chest,
wings in the solar plexus, goose bumps
riding the arms. A warmth like bronze
and then a hint of burning leaves—
smoke—something out there
wants to be near the soul that is mine
and it has a name. I have never
thought of God with any sense
of homecoming. Maybe you haven't either.
Now I seem to have woven us into this dance
between frost and fire. Maybe the silence
that holds me at bay from
what I've been told is the Divine
is the silence that fills my word.

Without Steel or Fire

      After lines by Jorge Luis Borges and Nicolás Guillén

Ever since school and even before
I have run my fingers along
the borders on maps. *To look at a river*
made of time and water is to see
the first cracks in the jigsaw
earth has become. Now inked lines
unfurl beneath my thumb, each boundary
an opportunity to straddle two countries at once,
to ride the vowels of two dialects.
I dream myself, beyond the stamps
on my passport, a citizen of the world
as though I were river carving its way
by persuasion alone, through rock.
I dream myself silt stirred up and rootless,
knowing the taste of each nation
through the root vegetables it yields.
Once Africa nestled right into
South America. Yam against yucca.
Now the river between them
is a sea that spans four time zones,
 its tireless fingers against the muscled earth
still working at the knots. I dream myself
harmless as the crane or butterfly
that travels thousands of miles to follow
the changing position of the sun,
irrefutable as the salmon that swims
upriver to spawn and die, their journeys
blurring even the fortified borders.

Juxtaposition
And The Gifts
Of Brilliant Surprise:
The Braided Poem

175

ESTRANGEMENT AND RECONCILIATION:

THE SELF HAS IT OUT WITH THE SELF

*T*he play of tension and resolution provides a viable structure for all poems, not to mention works in every other literary genre. Traditional plot structure relies on a building of tension. Adding the play of disconnection and disconnection to the conflict-dependent paradigm of the Freytag Pyramid opens the way for the ebb and flow of feeling as well as of event, giving us even more options with which to add and then resolve the tension that is necessary for allowing any work to end at some distance from where it began. Claudia Johnson first offered the terms "connection" and "disconnection" as essential to a less vertical, more horizontal notion of plot in her essay, *The Other Half of the Story*, which appeared in **The AWP Chronicle** in the mid-1990's and later was incorporated in a new edition of Janet Burroway's seminal textbook, **Writing Fiction**. I have found her terms particularly well suited to the lyric poem in which most of the "action" takes place inside the speaker and results in insight, or revelation, as opposed to resolution.

What follows is an exercise I adapted from a psychologist friend who used it as a means to help people gain insight about themselves. When I tried it as a poetry exercise, I had too much fun to keep it to myself. And it takes on further dimension if one agrees with Johnson's observations concerning the "horizontal plot."

Imagine two or more sides of yourself as distinct characters, each with reasons to be angry at, and to love or need, the other part(s). Write a poem in sections in which each side speaks or writes a letter to the other, letting tension (anger or bewilderment, perhaps) and then resolution (compromise, reconciliation, appreciation, full-blown affection) provide direction and a sense of discovery.

Remember to treat each voice as a character; i.e., to see parts of yourself as distinct entities, which will give you the freedom to invent, exaggerate, and play with material that could otherwise bog down in muddy introspection. You can have one side write a letter to the other and then have the other answer, or you could have several voices speak one at a time in a back-and-forth argument or roundtable discussion.

When I tried this, I made each side of myself address the other in letter form, one letter apiece, moving from resentment to appreciation. I also gave myself, as speaker in both instances, plenty of room to invent material so that the addressee of each letter became a caricature rather than anything that really resembled a side of me. I found myself exaggerating with great pleasure, mining imaginary material hoarded from several different times and sources, and ended up feeling liberated from my actual self while working on the poem. This is an exercise, then, that lets you out of yourself and in again by the back door, allowing you to mythologize yourself a little, which is powerful and often healing, an exercise not just in writing but in knowing the self a little better.

One Side Writes to the Other

Miss Homebody, Little Chicken, keep
a light for me by the window.
I need to be in the weather again.
I need to go deeper this time, where no
wall or roof will hold my silence.
I need a lantern strong enough to bring
the moon to eye level, and water enough
to keep me from thinking of water. I need
to crawl into myself as animal, all heartbeat
and heat, when the night thickens
with rain and slowed time.

I need to sit by a fire until I've
felt my way along every wall
of me, the cobwebs and bonepiles
and fertile caves. I need to find
once and for all the high pass that keeps
moving north and sending me back
out of breath and shaking ice from my hair,
sending me back with nothing in my hands
and nothing in my canyon heart, my name
beating against my teeth. Then
I want to dance until my own
feet drumming the ground
weave circle and flame, soil
and blood, a body to hold my dance.

Always you have drawn me home
with candlelight and ginger tea.
You have covered my chapped hands
and said *No one loves you like I do.*
You have coaxed ivy to flow up the sides
of this house and filled the rooms
with flutes, the smell of cinnamon, the pride
of tending what is ours. You have left
books for me everywhere, and said

*Estrangement
And Reconciliation:
The Self Has It
Out With The Self*

You're the only one I can talk to.
Still, something keeps falling from the sky
too thickly for words, falls like
buckshot or knives, and I see
it's only water. I am flesh.

I am flesh. This is what makes you
shiver, seeing me set off like before
in nothing but skin and my longing
for touch—for a lover's touch to flare
into nights I can melt down
in my mouth, in my palms, and then place
around you like a circle of polished stones.
You would forget all that, pull your cap
over your ears, and light incense
that smells of English gardens—
I want to let my hair grow wild.

I want to feel the wind tear through it
again, but this time I've packed
whatever in me has waited this long to surface
as pick and fuse to loosen old rock
and a rope that will stretch
anywhere, tied to the end of your chair.

And she answers:

Little soldier, dervish dancer,
puller of roots—I can't see you
growing old. Your future is a winter field,
stripped and brown if I look too hard, so I
pour another cup and fill the house with music
that weaves the air into petals and silks.
Sometimes your face softens, and your eyes
turn away from the window—how I've wanted
you to rest in the bower I've made.
When you pace, the page in my hand

turns to a powder of ink and dried wings.
When your voice grows ragged
with questions, I let our soup grow cold.
When you sit on the porch and stare
for hours at clouds foaming over the mountain
like a wave about to crest, this house
chokes me. I want to fill my lungs and howl.
I fill the saucer beneath each jade plant
and lie down to watch the leaves
fatten and shine.

You go away too much.
You're afraid of stillness
and cannot sleep through the night
but when you come home dazed and chattering,
your hair smelling of sage and your cheek gritty
with tears, when you pull from your pockets bright
peridot and quartz, when you step from your boots
to show me the brave pirouettes shown you
by someone you loved forever
for a while, these rooms
grow golden around you.

Then what I've read or thought all day
fills me with the stories
I've been waiting to love again.
My hand eases the blade through bread, rippling
with candlelight, its skin
suddenly strokable and fine as marble.
I open the garnet wine. Our laughter
starts slowly, then rings from the walls.
Among the apple peels and cheese rinds, sweet
crumbs and crystal, we pass the night
trading secrets and dozing
in one another's arms—your with your flint edges
and musk, me with my omnivorous eyes
that take you in until they darken and shine.

NOTES ON REVISION

We don't have to know what our piece is about at the outset—we *discover* its meaning or meanings while playing with it, opening ourselves to its possibilities—in other words, *revising.* Revising can be just as generative, just as "creative," as working in the middle of that first storm of words and ideas and moments. It's where we begin to listen to our own piece and let it offer us its possibilities. If, in the process, we feel ourselves being taken by surprise and saying things we didn't know we had in us, we know we have a keeper.

I'll begin with considerations related to the overall arc of a piece. If you're not sure where a piece is going, or if it's going, some of these terms might be useful.

Tension/resolution—There is always some form of tension in any finished piece, whether it's in the content or the structure or both. And "resolution" can take the form of revelation or of greater but somehow informative *ir*resolution. But the classic form of this is the Freytag Pyramid, for a long time the paradigm for plot structure, in which tension builds to a climax, after which a new situation or new knowledge results.

Notes On Revision

Disconnection/connection—Another form of tension/resolution which allows for the life and play of emotion, the human need for connection, or just the arrival at a new sensation or form of knowledge from a prior sense of confusion. There are many ways to look at the play of disconnection and connection. Think about it in relation to your favorite stories, novels, and poems, and see how it acts. It's a very basic dynamic, under our noses all the time but only relatively recently emphasized in the fine essay by Claudia Johnson I mentioned previously, *The Other Side of the Story*.

Movement—Usually meditative, towards a **revelation** or **epiphany**. Lyric poems do this—the action is in the movement of the mind/imagination rather than in a sequence of physical events

Raising and answering of questions—A central one or several.

Self-argument—Perhaps your piece is of two minds, and perhaps they both have a role.

Forceful or wistful or emphatic address to someone else—This can be an argument with someone else. Or the conveying of a secret to someone else. Sometimes the voice of your rough draft might suggest this direction.

Titles and last lines—Titles can set or state the intention of a piece, or can give crucial information to help ground the reader, thereby liberating the piece to travel quite far from its origins and take the reader with it. Titles sometimes, not always, do well to answer the "who, what, when, where" questions at the outset when a piece doesn't want to clunk itself up with that information. This can calm the reader and position her for travel. Other times a title can add whole new dimension, a metaphorical dimension, to a piece. I have given the example of Jack Gilbert's little parable, *In Dispraise of Poetry*, earlier in this book.

The right kind of **closure** can provoke a reader slightly beyond the physical ending of the piece. Sometimes it's interesting to see if a line somewhere in the middle or latter half of your rough draft feels like an "arrival" of sorts, a kind of high point, and then see how the other elements might be arranged/deleted/developed to work towards that arrival.

Emotional core—This is essential and hard to paraphrase or define. It's something we feel intuitively, in the gut, the experience of emotion as it arises from the piece.

These arc-related terms might help you discover an overall structure for your piece. Here are some more immediate considerations, to help the piece begin to feel a little less rough to you in the very first stages of revision:

Patterns—Can you see recurring images or textures or colors? Recurring phrases or sounds? Might you build on them, our might you do better to add texture by breaking up those patterns a little? Sometimes these patterns can help you detect an emerging voice or mood. Or perhaps a format, like a list.

Resonant places that might be developed further. Places where there seems to be more potential bubbling beneath the surface. Get another reader to help you identify these, but you can do this on your own as well, especially if you're more in your right brain than your left. Monitor your sensations as you read through your work.

Dead wood—Are there places where your language became abstract, predictable, trying too hard to interpret the material for the reader? I call these "low-energy" places. Try deleting them, and see what kind of new chemistry arises between the stronger parts. Also, what's left unsaid can make what is said look all the more deliberate and important, and is often implied by that stronger material.

Juxtaposition—This is great for energizing your language and perception. When you move things around so that they occur in unexpected combinations or sequences, you help them bounce off each other in provocative ways. Sometimes simple deletion can do this.

This probably should have come first in this second list. What are the **most alive bits of writing** in your draft? Get someone else to tell you. Put your piece aside, and then take yourself by surprise a day or two later. Highlight them, and then see if they can take you and the piece somewhere.

Remember, revision can be just as creative and generative as writing from the "storm." Relax. Be patient. Show up often. Listen to yourself as though listening to someone else. Have fun.

REFERENCES

A "Dark Star" Passes Through It

1. James Tate, *Consumed*, **The Oblivion Ha-Ha** (Boston: Little, Brown, & Company, 1970), 44.
2. Mary Oliver, *Beside the Waterfall*, **White Pine** (New York: Harcourt Brace & Company, 1994), 6-7.
3. James Wright, *Lying in a Hammock at Jim Duffy's Farm in Pine Island, Minnesota*, **Contemporary American Poetry**, Sixth Edition, ed., A. Poulin Jr. (Boston: Houghton Mifflin Company, 1996), 637.
4. William Stafford, *Traveling Through the Dark*, Ibid, 563-4.
5. Adrienne Rich, *The Loser*, **Snapshots of a Daughter-in-Law** (New York: W.W. Norton & Co., 1963), 15-17.

Towards A Poetics Of Pull-And-Release

1. Jack Gilbert, *In Dispraise of Poetry*, **Collected Poems** (New York: Alfred A. Knopf, 2012), 3.
2. Mary Ruefle, *From Memory*, **Life Without Speaking** (Tuscaloosa: University of Alabama Press, 1987), 13.
3. Sandra McPherson, *On a Picture of My Parents Together in Second Grade*, **The Year of Our Birth** (New York: The Ecco Press, 1978), 10-11.

4. Gaston Bachelard, *On Poetic Imagination and Reverie*, ed., Colette Gaudin (New York: Bobbs-Merrill Company, Inc., 1971), xiii.

5. Ibid, xix.

6. Ibid.

7. Susan Sontag, *On Style, Against Interpretation* (New York: Farrar, Strauss & Giroux, 1966), 22.

The "Personal" Poem As Sacred Space

1. Alicia Ostriker, *Stealing the Language* (Boston: Beacon Press, 1986), 6.

2. Linda Pastan, *Self Portrait, Carnival Evening* (New York: W.W. Norton, 1997), 24.

3. *Snowstorm*, Ibid, 14.

4. *Balance*, Ibid, 251.

5. *The Laws of Primogeniture*, Ibid, 280.

6. *Who Is It Accuses Us?*, Ibid, 132.

7. *You Are Odysseus*, Ibid, 72.

8. Jack Gilbert, *Betrothed, The Great Fires* (New York: Alfred A. Knopf, 1994), 29.

9. *Going Wrong*, Ibid, 3.

10. *Measuring the Tyger*, Ibid, 7.

11. *Recovering Amid The Farms*, Ibid, 22.

12. *The Lord Sits With Me Out In Front,* Ibid, 50.

13. *The History of Men*, Ibid, 52.

14. Jane Kenyon, *The Guest, Otherwise* (St. Paul: Graywolf Press, 1996), 160.

15. *Frost Flowers*, Ibid, 80.

16. *A Boy Goes Into the World*, Ibid, 147.

17. William Stafford, *At the Chairman's Housewarming, The Way It Is* (St. Paul: Graywolf Press, 1998), 113.

18. *Lit Instructor*, Ibid, 87.

19. *Thinking About Being Called Simple by a Critic*, Ibid, 213.

20. *Something That Happens Right Now*, Ibid, 8.

21. *A Little Gift*, Ibid, 135.

22. *A Ritual to Read to Each Other*, Ibid, 75.

23. *At the Bomb Testing Site*, Ibid, 67.

24. *Is This Feeling About the West Real?,* Ibid, 175.

25. Ibid, 176.

26. *When I Met My Muse*, Ibid, 222.

A Spiral Walk Through The Golden Mean

1. John Frederick Nims and David Mason, *An Introduction to Poetry*, Fourth Edition (New York: McGraw Hill, 2000), 242.
2. Ibid, 290.
3. Phyllis Levin, *Introduction*, *The Penguin Book of the Sonnet*, ed., Phyllis Levin (New York: Penguin Books, 2001), xxxvii.
4. Ibid, xxxviii.
5. Ibid, xxxvii.
6. Ibid.
7. Ibid.
8. Ibid, xxxviii.
9. Ibid.
10. Ibid.
11. William Stafford, *Time*, *Stories That Could Be True* (New York: Harper & Row, 1977).
12. William Stafford, *A Way of Writing*, *Claims for Poetry*, ed., Donald Hall (Ann Arbor: University of Michigan Press, 2001), 451.
13. Phyllis Levin, *Introduction*, *The Penguin Book of the Sonnet*, ed., Phyllis Levin (New York: Penguin Books, 2001), xxxix.
14. Ibid.
15. John Frederick Nims and David Mason, *Western Wind: An Introduction to Poetry*, Fourth Edition (New York: McGraw Hill, 2001), 293.
16. Paul Lake, *The Shape of Poetry, Part I*, *Expansive Poetry and Music Online*, October 2, 2010, http://home.earthlink.net~arthur505/lake1.html.
17. Ibid.
18. Ibid.
19. Ibid.
20. Ibid.
21. Charlotte Lackner Doyle, *The Creative Process: A Study in Paradox*, *Essays from Sarah Lawrence Faculty*, Vol. 3, No. 1, 1975.
22. Ibid.
23. Ibid.

"All The Softness Truth Requires:" Speculation As Invitation And Persuasion

1. Elizabeth Bishop, *In the Waiting Room*, **Geography III** (New York: Farrar, Straus & Giroux, 1971), 3-8.

2. Robert Hayden, *Those Winter Sundays*, **Contemporary American Poetry**, Sixth Edition, ed., A. Poulin Jr. (Boston, Houghton Mifflin Company, 1996), 216.

3. Betsy Sholl, *After That*, **Late Psalm** (Madison: University of Wisconsin Press, 2004), 47-48.

4. Stanley Kunitz, *The Abduction*, **Passing Through** (New York/London, W. W. Norton & Company, 1995), 113-114.

5. Robert Creeley, *I Know a Man*, **Contemporary American Poetry**, Sixth Edition, ed., A. Poulin Jr. (Boston: Houghton Mifflin Company, 1996), 85.

6. Pattiann Rogers, *The Importance of the Whale in a Field of Iris*, **The Firekeeper** (Minneapolis: Milkweed Editions, 1994), 139.

7. *When at Night*, Ibid, 153.

8. Denise Levertov, *The Wings*, http://www.angelfire.com/ca/iloveDave/mydl. html.

9. William Stafford, *Lit Instructor*, **The Way It Is** (St. Paul: Graywolf Press, 1998), 87.

Press Send: Risk, Intuition, And The Transparent Poem

1. Ron Padgett, *Walking With Walt*, **How Long** (Minneapolis: Coffee House Press, 2011), 13.

2. Frank O'Hara, *Personism: A Manifesto*, **The Selected Poems of Frank O'Hara**, ed., Donald Allen (New York: Vintage Books, 1974), xiii.

3. Ibid.

4. Ibid.

5. Frank O'Hara, *Poetry*, **The Selected Poems of Frank O'Hara**, ed., Donald Allen (New York: Vintage Books, 1974), 18-19.

6. Ibid., xiv.

7. William Stafford, *A Little Gift*, **The Way It Is** (St. Paul: Graywolf Press, 1998), 135.

8. William Stafford, *A Way of Writing*, **Claims for Poetry**, ed., Donald Hall (Ann Arbor: The University of Michigan Press, 2001), 450.

9. Frank O'Hara, *Why I Am Not a Painter*, **The Selected Poems of Frank O'Hara**, ed., Donald Allen (New York: Vintage Books, 1974), 112.

10. ***Robert Motherwell and the New York School: Storming the Citadel***, a film by Catherine Tatge (Long Beach: Kultur). (Date of production not given).

11. Ibid.

12. Ibid.

13. Robert Creeley, *On the Road: Notes on Artists and Poets, 1950-65*, **Claims for Poetry**, ed., Donald Hall (Ann Arbor: The University of Michigan Press, 2001), 62.

14. Ibid., 62-63.

15. Ibid., 64.

16. Ibid.

17. Robert Creeley, *The Window*, **Contemporary American Poetry**, Sixth Edition, ed., A. Poulin Jr. (Boston: Houghton Mifflin Company, 1996), 91.

18. Denise Levertov, *Some Notes on Organic Form*, **The Poet in the World** (New York: New Directions, 1973), 11.

19. Denise Levertov, *Stepping Westward*, **Contemporary American Poetry**, Sixth Edition, ed., A. Poulin Jr. (Boston: Houghton Mifflin Company, 1996), 309.

20. William Stafford, *A Way of Writing*, **Claims for Poetry**, ed., Donald Hall (Ann Arbor: The University of Michigan Press, 2001), 451.

21. Ibid.

22. William Stafford, *When I Met My Muse*, **The Way It Is** (St. Paul: Graywolf Press, 1998), 222.

23. W.S. Merwin, *The Moon Before Morning*, (Port Townsend, Copper Canyon Press, 2014), 118.

BIBLIOGRAPHY

Bachelard, Gaston, *On Poetic Imagination and Reverie*, ed., Colette Gaudin, New York: Bobbs-Merrill Company, Inc., 1971.

Bachelard, Gaston, *The Poetics of Reverie*, translated by Daniel Russell, Boston: Beacon Press, 1971.

Bishop, Elizabeth, *Geography III*, New York: Farrar, Straus & Giroux, 1971.

Doyle, Charlotte Lackner, *Essays from Sarah Lawrence Faculty*, Vol. 3, No. 1, 1975.

Gilbert, Jack, *Collected Poems*, New York: Alfred A. Knopf, 2012.

Gilbert, Jack, *The Great Fires*, New York: Alfred A. Knopf, 1994.

Hall, Donald, ed., *Claims for Poetry*, Ann Arbor: University of Michigan Press, 2001.

Kenyon, Jane, *Otherwise*, St. Paul: Graywolf Press, 1996.

Kunitz, Stanley, *Passing Through*, New York: W.W. Norton & Company, 1995.

Lake, Paul, *Expansive Poetry and Music Online*, http://home.earthlink.net~arthur505/lake1.html.

Levertov, Denise, *Poems 1960-1967*, New York: New Directions, 1967.

Levertov, Denise, *The Poet in the World*, New York: New Directions, 1973.

Levin, Phyllis, *The Penguin Book of the Sonnet*, New York: Penguin Books, 2001.

McPherson, Sandra, *The Year of Our Birth*, New York: The Ecco Press, 1978.

Merwin, W.S., *The Moon Before Morning*, Port Townsend: Copper Canyon Press, 2014.

Nims, John Fredrick and David Mason, *An Introduction to Poetry, Fourth Edition*, New York: McGraw Hill, 2000.

O'Hara, Frank, *The Selected Poems of Frank O'Hara*, ed., Donald Allen, New York: Vintage Books, 1974.

Oliver, Mary, *White Pine*, New York: Harcourt Brace & Company, 1994.

Ostriker, Alicia, *Stealing the Language*, Boston: Beacon Press, 1986.

Padgett, Ron, *How Long*, Minneapolis: Coffee House Press, 2011.

Pastan, Linda, *Carnival Evening*, New York: W.W. Norton, 1997.

Poulin, A. Jr., ed., *Contemporary American Poetry*, Sixth Edition, Boston: Houghton, Mifflin Company, 1996.

Rich, Adrienne, *Snapshots of a Daughter-in-Law*, New York: W. W. Norton & Company, 1963.

Rogers, Pattiann, *The Firekeeper*, Minneapolis: Milkweed Editions, 1994.

Ruefle, Mary, *Life Without Speaking*, Tuscaloosa: University of Alabama Press, 1987.

Sholl, Betsy, *Late Psalm*, Madison: University of Wisconsin Press, 2004.

Sontag, Susan, *Against Interpretation*, New York: Farrar, Strauss & Giroux, 1966.

Stafford, William, *Stories That Could Be True*, New York: Harper & Row, 1977.

Stafford, William, *The Way It Is*, St. Paul: Graywolf Press, 1998.

Tate, James, *The Oblivion Ha-Ha*, Boston: Little, Brown, & Company, 1970.

ACKNOWLEDGMENTS

The author would like to thank the editors of the following journals and book in which these essays first appeared, often in earlier versions.

The Writers Chronicle: Towards A Poetics Of Pull-And-Release: Some Thoughts On Silence In Poems; The "Personal" Poem As Sacred Space; A Spiral Walk Through The Golden Mean; Press Send: Risk, Intuition, And The Transparent Poem.

Southern Indiana Review (second publication, *Numéro Cinq*): *A "Dark Star" Passes Through It.*

Poetry East: A Meditation On Place, Real And Imagined.

Poet Lore: "All the Softness Truth Requires:" Speculation As Invitation And Persuasion.

The Practice of Poetry: Writing Exercises From Poets Who Teach: One Side Writes To The Other.

Poetry International: From Nymph to Elder: Beyond The Viability of Seduction.

Iron Horse Literary Review: First Lines By Others: A Leap Into Fruitful Spaces.

PERMISSIONS

ABOUT THE AUTHOR

Leslie Ullman taught for twenty-seven years at University of Texas-El Paso where she directed the Creative Writing Program and established the Bilingual MFA Program. She still teaches in the low-residency MFA Program in Writing at Vermont College of the Fine Arts where she has been a faculty member since 1981. She is the author of four collections of poetry. Her awards include the Yale Series of Younger Poets Prize, the Iowa Poetry Prize, the New Mexico/Arizona Book Award, and two NEA Fellowships. She and her husband Erik live in Taos, New Mexico.

ALSO BY 3: A TAOS PRESS

Collecting Life: Poets on Objects Known and Imagined
Madelyn Garner and Andrea Watson

Seven
Sheryl Luna

The Luminosity
Bonnie Rose Marcus

Trembling in the Bones: A Commemorative Edition
Eleanor Swanson

3 A.M.
Phyllis Hotch

Ears of Corn: Listen
Max Early

Elemental
Bill Brown

Rootwork
Veronica Golos

Farolito
Karen S. Córdova

Godwit
Eva Hooker

The Ledgerbook
William S. Barnes

The Mistress
Catherine Strisik